# THE
# MODERN POETS' WORLD

## THE POETRY BOOKSHELF

*General Editor:* JAMES REEVES

Selected Poems of D. H. Lawrence

Selected Poems of John Donne

Selected Poems of John Clare

Selected Poems of Robert Browning

Selected Poems of William Blake
*edited by F. W. Bateson*

English and Scottish Ballads
*edited by Robert Graves*

Selected Poems of William Wordsworth
*edited by Roger Sharrock*

The Modern Poets' World

\*

*Also by James Reeves*
The Poets' World
*An annotated anthology of English Poetry
from Anglo-Saxon times to the XXth century*

# THE
# MODERN POETS' WORLD

*Edited with an Introduction
and Commentary
by*

## JAMES REEVES

WILLIAM HEINEMANN LTD
MELBOURNE :: LONDON :: TORONTO

FIRST PUBLISHED 1957

Published by
William Heinemann Ltd
99 Great Russell Street, London, W.C.1
Printed by Morrison and Gibb Ltd
London and Edinburgh

# CONTENTS

# INTRODUCTION

The first important thing about contemporary literature is that it *is* contemporary: it is speaking to us and for us, here, now. Judgment can only follow an act of sympathy and understanding, and to let our appreciation grow outwards from that which immediately appeals to us is both wiser and more enjoyable than to echo the judgments of others or to restrict and sour our appreciation by hastily attacking anything which at first seems difficult or irritating.

THESE are the concluding words of Michael Roberts' introduction to the first *Faber Book of Modern Verse*, which appeared twenty years ago. Himself a poet, Roberts was a critic and editor of discernment, and it is appropriate to recall his words today, since they are no less true now than when he wrote them. Indeed, they need saying even more. Roberts wrote of the hostility towards modern poetry which then prevailed; but the attitude to-day is less one of hostility than one of apathy. A knowledge of the poetry of his time was once part of an educated man's mental luggage; now it is not. Most people, even intelligent and educated people, travel through life without knowing or caring anything about modern poetry—or for that matter, any poetry. They do not feel the loss. If they travel the lighter, who can *prove* that they are the poorer? Yet, as Roberts said, contemporary poetry can help us to understand contemporary life, provided we are ready to approach it with sympathy. If we ask modern poetry to show us modern life, in all its complexity and perplexity, and if we are prepared to give it our ear and our understanding, it will not fail us. It must be admitted that in the divorce between poetry and the reading public—to say nothing of the enormous listening and viewing public that has

xiii

come into being during our time—both parties have suffered. As the public has become indifferent, poetry has become specialised. For the good of both sides, it is important that the breach should be mended. Not for a generation—two generations, some would say—has any serious poet felt able to appeal to a large public. In some respects this has had a bad effect on poetry; yet the modern poet, who can scarcely expect to write for any but other poets, still feels that he has something to say, if not to the masses, at any rate to a wide audience of educated readers, provided they will attend with sympathy and patience. To the poet, life is meaningless without poetry; he is dismayed to find that most people can manage to live without it. It puts him in a class apart, and he would prefer to feel that he is, after all, in Wordsworth's phrase, 'a man speaking to men'. The possibility that the world may have finished with poetry for ever simply does not occur to him. There has probably never yet been a civilisation without poetry of some sort. Can twentieth-century man be the first to attempt such a civilisation? If poetry has meant something to men of all previous ages, how can the twentieth century do without it?

In considering the function of poetry in relation to modern life, it is worth while to ponder these words of D. H. Lawrence:

> The sheer delight of a child's apperception is based on *wonder*; and deny it as we may, knowledge and wonder counteract one another. So that, as knowledge increases, wonder decreases. We say again: familiarity breeds contempt. So that as we grow older, and become more familiar with phenomena, we become more contemptuous of them. But that is only partly true. It has taken some races of men thousands of years to become contemptuous of the moon, and to the Hindu the cow is still wondrous. It is not familiarity that breeds contempt: it is the assumption of knowledge. Anybody who looks at the moon and says, 'I know all about that poor orb', is, of course, bored by the moon.
>
> Now the great and fatal fruit of our civilisation, which is a civilisation based on knowledge and hostile to experience, is boredom. All our wonderful education and learning is producing

a grand sum total of boredom. Modern people are inwardly thoroughly bored. Do as they may, they are bored.

They are bored because they experience nothing. And they experience nothing because the wonder has gone out of them. And when the wonder has gone out of a man he is dead. He is henceforth only an insect.[1]

It might seem at first sight that Lawrence is setting up a simple opposition between science and poetry, knowledge and wonder. But elsewhere he makes it clear that he has no objection to science so long as it is concerned with discovery and not the mere systematisation of facts. The danger of science, as the main intellectual preoccupation of the age, is that it is becoming so specialised that the spirit of discovery—that is, of wonder— is being squeezed out; it is becoming arid and fact-ridden. It is growing sophisticated, and to some modern scientists the naïve enquiring spirit that animated such discoverers as Boyle and Darwin and Faraday must seem sadly amateur, perhaps even quaint. We are all growing sophisticated; we mistrust the emotion of wonder, the idea of magic. These things are truly child-like, and we think of them as childish. Sophistication is the enemy of poetry, even though poetry itself has become sophisticated. But as Lawrence said, if we lose wonder, the sense of magic, the thirst for experience, we become bored. Boredom is a state on the way to death.

Even if it be granted that we need to retain our sense of wonder, it may still be objected that we do not need poetry. There is the cinema, there is the radio and television, there is science fiction—surely all these satisfy the need for magic. Will not sport, travel, dancing satisfy our need for experience much more directly than poetry? Anyway, thousands of books are published every year for millions of readers. What does it matter that few of them are poetry?

One of the poems in this collection, *The Animals* by Edwin Muir, deals with the idea that language is the distinguishing mark of man; we use words not only to record our experience,

---

[1] *D. H. Lawrence: Selected Literary Criticism* (Heinemann)

to preserve it against loss, we use it to communicate it to others. The need to preserve and to communicate our experience is basic to man's nature. Perhaps this is because we feel our experience more intensely than the animals; our wonder and joy at the beauty of the world, our fear at being lonely, our grief at losing someone we love, our delight in physical pleasure—all these and other emotions are so intense that they are scarcely complete unless they are expressed in words: it is as if our most precious experience needs to be communicated in order to be fully realised. There are, of course, other means of self-expression—music and the plastic arts, for instance—but words are the most universal medium. All men employ language, and all experience, from the most commonplace to the most memorable, can find expression in words.

As Lawrence says, we must experience if we are to live. But we cannot live by experience alone; only the animals can do that. When poets or philosophers speak of a 'return to nature', that is usually what they mean—an attempt to regain something of animal experience in an age that has become too sophisticated, too rational. But as men, we need not only to experience but also to apprehend our experience. We need not only to live but also to understand life. Not even the most unthinking of savages attempts to live without some effort to understand life, to formulate rules for living, methods of crossing the space which divides one mind from another.

We cannot apprehend experience by reason alone, though in a scientific age that is what we tend to attempt. Our feelings need expression too. Religion is an attempt to understand life both rationally and emotionally: when it becomes either too rational or too emotional, it loses support. Poetry has, in most civilisations, been a means of apprehending experience both rationally and emotionally. Not everyone feels the need to apprehend his experience by writing poetry, but nearly all children take delight in hearing or reading it. A poet's job, like that of any other working member of society, is to do for others what they cannot do for themselves. A poet employs a tailor to make him clothes; a tailor, if he is interested in such things, employs poets to put into words his feelings at the beauty of the spring, the unrest of being in love, or the sadness of death. Not only can poetry, as the saying is, 'relieve his feelings'; it can enrich all his experience by suggesting aspects of it which he would otherwise have missed. To put it simply, a man who has read much poetry, and remembers some of it, will get more out of life than one who tries to do without it altogether, because everything he sees and hears and feels has been seen and heard and felt by poets, and it has been their business to express all this in the best possible language, the most pleasing and the most permanent. Is there something special about western man in the twentieth century that enables him to dispense with poetry and what poetry can give?

To what I have been saying it might be objected that we have, in a sense, grown out of poetry; that poetry has nothing new to say; that poets have been at it a long time, this business of interpreting experience, and that if they have not done it as well as possible by now, they never will do it. Now while the basic nature of man and his experience may change very slowly, if at all, the forms which his experience takes vary continually from age to age. The view man takes of his experience, the importance he attaches to this or that aspect of it, is for ever changing; and these changes are expressed in poetry, as well as in the arts. In architecture, for instance, a Gothic cathedral expresses what we call the spirit of the middle ages, just as a Georgian country house or a Victorian town hall expresses a different spirit. In English poetry a fifteenth-century ballad, an Elizabethan love sonnet, an eighteenth-century satire, a Victorian historical poem, and a twentieth-century lyric all express in some degree the differing experience of men in different ages.

In approaching modern poetry, the reader is asked to make an effort of sympathy—sympathy not merely for the poet, but for the age in which he lives, of which poetry is only one manifestation. What he must remember has been well expressed by Abraham Cowley, a poet of an earlier and in some ways a similar age:

> A warlike, various, and a tragical age is best to write of, but worst to write in.

If ever there was a 'warlike, various, and a tragical age', it is the twentieth century. We have endured the two worst wars in history, and appear to be preparing for the next; we have made unprecedented progress in science and technology; revolutions in thought have taken place in almost every sphere; the nearer we get to the realisation of prosperity and happiness for the mass of mankind, the more certainly are our hopes dashed by some new and unexpected crisis, military, political or economic. No sooner have we conquered one disease than we are threatened by another; no sooner do we achieve one end in politics for which we have long striven than it turns out not to be what we were looking for after all. The surer our means of achieving almost any end we desire, the less certain we become of what we desire or ought to desire. We proclaim as our political purposes 'freedom from want', 'freedom from fear', 'freedom of speech', 'freedom of religion', and it turns out that what we have gained is freedom to say nothing worth saying, freedom to stay away from the church of our choice, freedom to look at a television set all day. If we begin to wonder *how* we are going to use our freedom, our increase of scientific and technological knowledge, our improved health and our increased leisure, then we have to think about the *quality* of living, and not just the quantity of the means to live.

That is where poetry comes in; but in judging modern poetry we must remember that we live in the most difficult of all times for poets, the 'warlike, various, and tragical' twentieth century.

Some of the poets whose work is printed in this book are concerned with the state of society, with politics, and with religion; others write of more private experiences; but all are concerned with the quality of their individual responses to their age. All are concerned with the quality of living. The age is one in which, whatever private and limited certainties we enjoy, we are collectively certain of nothing—nothing, that is, except our personal identities. We are uncertain of the past, for history and archaeology are continually modifying our accepted ideas; we are uncertain of the future; we are uncertain of the metaphysical and religious bases of life; we tend, therefore, to group oursleves about this or that religious or political or scientific flag in order to have the comfort of not being alone. We allow some group idea to determine our thinking and even order our lives for us —socialism, Catholicism, materialism, the British Empire, the American way of life. The area of experience in which we exercise a power of choice, in which we think and act and feel as individuals and not as members of a group, is very limited. It may be argued that for the mass of mankind this was always so. But the religious and political ideals on which our civilisation is founded demand that this should be continually increased for as many people as possible. The value of the poet to society is that he has always insisted as much as possible on his right to personal identity. He is the individualist; he reserves the right to think and feel for himself. And of this insistence his poetry is the product.

It may be that modern man is losing the desire for individual living and prefers to take shelter with a group. Certainly both Russian and American collectivism threaten the survival of the individual, the person who can think and act and feel for himself. The volume of mass thinking has grown alarmingly with the perfection of mass communication. If this is so, then the salt has lost its savour; a savourless existence is not worth having.

In these circumstances the poet has a function of peculiar importance. Here, of course, I include the artist, in whatever medium. It is his especial duty to keep his responses to experience fresh and vital, to refuse to be submerged by any group, to refuse to surrender his identity. Modern poetry is, among other things, the account of how modern poets have tried to do this. The way in which a poet practises his personal identity and maintains himself amidst the distractions of the world, usually appears in the way in which he conceives of the technique of poetry; in other words, he is concerned with the kind of man he is, and that means the kind of poem he writes, and that means its subject-matter, its vocabulary, its rhythm and metre—or in the narrow sense, its form.

Michael Roberts distinguished between two main types of modern poet—those who, like Pound and Eliot, ally themselves with a continental tradition and assimilate foreign influence, especially French; and those who, like Blunden and Muir and Graves, carry on the native English tradition. The former came from America, like the Imagist movement they imported into England before World War I; yet not all Americans are cosmopolitan. Frost came to England to learn the writing of poetry in company with such very English poets as Edward Thomas and Wilfred Gibson; Ransom, another American, is almost pedantically 'English' in form and diction.

English-born poets whose work is mainly traditional in form are W. H. Davies, Housman and Flecker; and among younger poets, Heath-Stubbs and Elizabeth Jennings. The more self-consciously experimental or 'modern' in style include Hopkins, Cummings, C. Day Lewis, Empson, MacNeice, Owen, Auden and Barker. Yet to define 'modernism' in terms of form and language would be superficial. The matter has been well expressed by an American poet, Hart Crane:

> I put no particular value on the simple objective of 'modernity'.
> . . . It seems to me that a poet will accidentally define his time well
> enough simply by reacting honestly and to the full extent of his
> sensibilities to the states of passion, experience and rumination that
> fate forces on him, first hand.

As for the subjects of modern poetry, it will be recalled that the twentieth century is, above all, a 'various' age—an age in which new fashions in every department of thought have replaced traditional conceptions. The systematic study of the human mind by the human mind which goes by the name of psychology, for instance, is reflected in the poems of Graves, Eliot, Auden, Spender and Empson; and no doubt it has modified the thinking of almost every poet of the period. The importance which psychology ascribes to childhood influences in the formation of character and temperament has led to an increased interest in this subject. This is reflected in poems by D. H. Lawrence, Dylan Thomas, Barker and Betjeman.

Direct expression of the public concerns of the time is not here widely represented—rather, the influence of outside events has been indirect. But Sassoon, Owen and Alun Lewis had a direct concern with war which profoundly affected their work. Gascoyne also reflects political crisis in a highly imaginative and, as it turned out, prophetic poem. Public affairs, and what might be called the outer world, also find a place in poems by Auden, Cameron, Enright and MacNeice.

Others are represented more by poems of inner conflict and private life: among these are Hardy, Edward Thomas, Blunden, Frost, and Sassoon. The world of non-human nature is the concern of poems by men as different as Campbell and Young.

One major theme which runs through much of the poetry of our time is that of man's primal innocence, in the spiritual sense. Poems by Yeats and Muir, Cummings, Dylan Thomas and Young reflect this preoccupation. In an age where we have the material means to achieve any desired end and where we have achieved such disastrous results, where knowledge has outrun experience, doubt certainty, power wisdom, it is natural that those who think and feel should be oppressed with a sense of guilt. Guilt for the past and anxiety for the future are ruling contemporary states of mind. It is inevitable that poets should have concerned themselves deeply and even desperately with the problem of lost innocence and the Fall of Man.

All these matters will be found considered in greater detail in the Commentary on individual poets and poems at the end of the book. All that can be established by such a summary discussion as the foregoing is that modern poetry is intimately connected with modern life; that the poets have been intimately and continuously concerned with the major problems of their age. It is not their business to write versified sermons or political discussions; there are pulpits and newspapers, periodicals and broadcasts for that. If one fact emerges more clearly than any other from this sketch of modern poetry, it is that the poet's first and best duty is to be himself, as fully and as characteristically as the world will let him. He cannot act for others, he cannot live for them; but he can and does show them how to feel.

The characteristics and groupings indicated above, incomplete and tentative as they are, serve to show how one poet can cut across all neat attempts at classification. For the reader of poetry, as distinct from the professional critic or literary historian, the enumeration of tendencies and the discovery of 'schools' is profitless. If 'poet' means anything, it means an individual. The curious reader may note that certain poets have been influenced by Eliot, others by Graves, others by Yeats or Dylan Thomas; such groupings give comfort to a certain type of mind that enjoys tidiness for its own sake, even at the risk of falsification. But if we wish to see modern poetry as it is, we must be prepared for its variety, for its lack of accepted rules, for the absence of a prevailing 'style' like the Augustan style of Pope and his followers. A rule, a tendency, a trend means nothing if it is the invention of critics and not felt as compelling by poets. A critic may delight to find that the young poet X is like Mr. Eliot, while X may have been trying desperately to be as unlike Eliot as possible. The business of the reader is to find out how far X is himself, and what he has to say which is personal and unique. The poets represented in this book are here, not because they are alike, but because they are different.

One of the charges most frequently levelled at modern poetry is that it is obscure. This, as an American poet, Randall Jarrell, has pointed out in a wise and persuasive essay,[1] is not so much a real charge as a measure of the divorce between poetry and the public. To those who have read no poetry at all, all poetry will at first seem obscure. There are editions of Milton and Gray in which *L'Allegro* and *The Bard*, each about one hundred and fifty lines long, are given twenty-five pages of explanatory notes apiece. To those who habitually read only the poetry of the nineteenth century and earlier, any characteristic modern poem may appear obscure; but for anyone who makes a habit of reading modern poetry, the obscurity is likely to disappear. It is no part of the modern poet's task to write poems like those of earlier ages; he must find new ways of expressing himself. Whenever poets have broken away from traditional conceptions of poetry, they have been found obscure by their own generation. This is inevitable, for what a modern poet in any period is doing is forming the consciousness, the sensibility, even the language of the next generation. You cannot expect to pick up a volume of contemporary poems at random and make sense of them by means of an intelligence formed by the thought and language of yesterday. Eliot is bound to seem difficult if you apply to his work the standards and methods by which you read Keats and Wordsworth—just as Keats and Wordsworth, in their time, were incomprehensible to readers accustomed to the language of Thomson and Pope. As Jarrell says:

> When you begin to read a poem you are entering a foreign country whose laws and language and life are a kind of translation of your own ; but to accept it because its stews taste exactly like your old mother's hash, or to reject it because the owl-headed goddess of wisdom in its temple is fatter than the Statue of Liberty, is an equal mark of that want of imagination, that inaccessibility to experience, of which each of us who dies a natural death will die.
>
> That the poetry of the first half of this century often *was* too difficult—just as the poetry of the eighteenth century *was* full of antitheses, that of the metaphysicals full of conceits, that of the

---

[1] 'The Obscurity of the Poet'—*Poetry and the Age* (Faber).

Elizabethan dramatists full of rant and quibbles—is a truism that it would be absurd to deny. How our poetry got this way—how romanticism was purified and exaggerated and 'corrected' into modernism; how poets carried all possible tendencies to their limits with more than scientific zeal; . . . how poet and public stared at each other with righteous indignation, till the poet said, 'Since you won't read me, I'll make sure you can't'—is one of the most complicated and interesting of stories. But Modernism was not 'that lion's den from which no tracks return', but only a sort of canvas whale from which Jonah after Jonah, throughout the late '20's and early '30's, made a penitent return, back to rhyme and metre and plain broad Statement.

In order to give the reader some help I have appended a commentary, sparing enough in places, and more detailed where it seemed necessary. I would ask teachers and others who find my comments superfluous to ignore them, and in doing so to remember those readers who may be studying this book privately, without any help from instruction or discussion. I have no wish to impose my own readings, or to offer any ready-made reactions as a substitute for the reader's efforts. One source of value in modern poetry may be its very difficulty. Unlike so much that is offered for entertainment, poetry demands mental effort, and this is one reason why the experience of poetry is worth acquiring. In passing rapidly from the style of one poet to that of another, however, as is inevitable in reading an anthology, the reader may find himself at a loss in making an immediate adjustment of his mental processes; and one object of the Commentary is to help him in making the adjustment. Moreover, the poets of this century have, with a few exceptions, written mainly short poems. This is no mere fashion, but goes deeper. In remarking the absence of significant long poems, some critics fail to realise that a number of short lyrics by a single poet may constitute what is in effect a long poem: in other words, they may represent successive stages in the poet's preoccupation with a single theme. In isolating one short poem, therefore, an anthologist may be detaching it from its context, and thus making it less accessible to comprehension. To remedy this, I have in my comments tried to relate such poems to the general context of the poet's work.

Any selection such as this is bound to be personal, yet I have taken pains that it should not be merely eccentric. I have read hundreds of poems in scores of volumes by dozens of poets before arriving at my selection; and I have considered with especial care those poets for whom I have no private predilection but who are generally judged to be important, or good, or representative. I laid down no arbitrary date-lines to govern inclusion or exclusion; the earliest poet represented, Emily Dickinson, was a mid-Victorian who, in my judgment, wrote out of her time, if she can be said to have written 'in' any time at all. Her poems, if they were to-day published for the first time, would appear just as modern as they ever were. As a technician, Hopkins too was born out of his time. Hardy is an essentially twentieth-century poet, though the greater part of his life fell in the nineteenth. Housman also is no Victorian in the sense that Tennyson and Browning were. The decision whether to include or exclude was in some cases not easy; the last thing I would claim is that this selection is even approximately definitive or authoritative. The compass of the book, quite apart from my own limitations, would not allow of that. A selection so small as this could only falsify if it attempted to be absolutely representative. All that could be looked for was a reasonably comprehensive and representative cross-section of modern poetry; as the selection took shape, it began to appear that three main requisites governed the choice of a poem: it had to be a representative poem by a poet whose work generally is representative and worthy of further study; it had to be comprehensible by the average reader as a detached unit of the poet's work; and it had to be of individual and intrinsic poetic interest and worth. In short, this is a collection to read, re-read, and enjoy for its own sake, rather than as a text-book of modern trends and tendencies.

While I feel sure that the older poets represented are among the most important and excellent of their time, I am inevitably on less sure ground the nearer I come to the present day. I do not claim that the poems by younger poets could not in some cases, with equal propriety, be replaced by others. Yet I feel confident that they are poems worth studying as expressions of the contemporary spirit, and that their writers have as good a chance of survival as any others of their generation. One mistake which I hope I have not made is to suppose it possible to look at the poetry of my time with the eyes of posterity. The anthologies which we make to-day of the poetry of the Romantic period have a very different look from those made at the time: if anyone claims that he can distinguish the Coleridge, the Keats, the Clare of to-day from the Barry Cornwall, the Mrs. Barbauld and the Mrs. Hemans, let him study the anthologies and the periodical criticism of the 1820's. It is my hope that the one hundred or so poems I have selected give a fair picture of the poetry of the first half of the twentieth century, and—more than this—that they can all be read and re-read with enjoyment by those whose acquaintance with modern poetry is as yet slight.

For help in the preparation of this volume I acknowledge with gratitude the help of my wife, of Mrs. Dorothy Glen, of Mr. Harold Morland, of Miss Angelica Zander, and of the staff of the National Book League's information service.

J. R.

*Chalfont St. Giles,*
1957

# POEMS

# W. H. AUDEN

## Who's Who

A shilling life will give you all the facts:
How Father beat him, how he ran away,
What were the struggles of his youth, what acts
Made him the greatest figure of his day:
Of how he fought, fished, hunted, worked all night,
Though giddy, climbed new mountains; named a sea:
Some of the last researchers even write
Love made him weep pints like you and me.

With all his honours on, he sighed for one                    *Failure at heart*
Who, say astonished critics, lived at home;
Did little jobs about the house with skill
And nothing else; could whistle; would sit still
Or potter round the garden; answered some
Of his long marvellous letters but kept none.

## Culture

Happy the hare at morning, for she cannot read
The Hunter's waking thoughts, lucky the leaf
Unable to predict the fall, lucky indeed
The rampant suffering suffocating jelly
Burgeoning in pools, lapping the grits of the desert,
But what shall man do, who can whistle tunes by heart,
Knows to the bar when death shall cut him short like the cry
    of the shearwater,
What can he do but defend himself from his knowledge?

How comely are his places of refuge and the tabernacles of his
    peace,
The new books upon the morning table, the lawns and the
    afternoon terraces!
Here are the playing-fields where he may forget his ignorance
To operate within a gentleman's agreement: twenty-two sins
    have here a certain license.
Here are the thickets where accosted lovers combatant
May warm each other with their wicked hands,
Here are the avenues for incantation and workshops for the
    cunning engravers.
The galleries are full of music, the pianist is storming the keys,
    the great cellist is crucified over his instrument,
That none may hear the ejaculations of the sentinels
Nor the sigh of the most numerous and the most poor; the
    thud of their falling bodies
Who with their lives have banished hence the serpent and the
    faceless insect.

## The Capital

Quarter of pleasures where the rich are always waiting,
Waiting expensively for miracles to happen,
O little restaurant where the lovers eat each other,
Café where exiles have established a malicious village;

You with your charm and your apparatus have abolished
The strictness of winter and the spring's compulsion;
Far from your lights the outraged punitive father,
The dullness of mere obedience here is apparent.

Yet with orchestras and glances, O, you betray us
To belief in our infinite powers; and the innocent
Unobservant offender falls in a moment
Victim to the heart's invisible furies.

In unlighted streets you hide away the appalling;
Factories where lives are made for a temporary use
Like collars or chairs, rooms where the lonely are battered
Slowly like pebbles into fortuitous shapes.

But the sky you illumine, your glow is visible far
Into the dark countryside, the enormous, the frozen,
Where, hinting at the forbidden like a wicked uncle,
Night after night to the farmer's children you beckon.

# GEORGE BARKER

## My Joy, my Jockey, my Gabriel

*(First Cycle of Love Poems: V)*

My joy, my jockey, my Gabriel
Who bares his horns above my sleep
Is sleeping now. And I shall keep him
In valley and on pinnacle
And marvellous in my tabernacle.

My peace is where his shoulder holds
My clouds among his skies of face;
His plenty is my peace, my peace:
And like a serpent by a boulder
His shade I rest in glory coiled.

Time will divide us, and the sea
Wring its sad hands all day between;
The autumn bring a change of scene.
But always and for ever he
At night will sleep and keep by me.

## To my Mother

Most near, most dear, most loved and most far,
Under the window where I often found her
Sitting as huge as Asia, seismic with laughter,
Gin and chicken helpless in her Irish hand,
Irresistible as Rabelais, but most tender for
The lame dogs and hurt birds that surround her,—
She is a procession no one can follow after
But be like a little dog following a brass band.

She will not glance up at the bomber, or condescend
To drop her gin and scuttle to a cellar,
But lean on the mahogany table like a mountain
Whom only faith can move, and so I send
O all my faith and all my love to tell her
That she will move from mourning into morning.

## JOHN BETJEMAN *gift of rhyme & metre. limited in range*

### Indoor Games near Newbury

In among the silver birches winding ways of tarmac wander
   And the signs to Bussock Bottom, Tussock Wood and Windy
     Brake,
Gabled lodges, tile-hung churches, catch the lights of our
   · Lagonda
   As we drive to Wendy's party, lemon curd and Christmas cake.

Rich the makes of motor whirring, past the pine-plantations
    purring
        Come up, Hupmobile, Delage!
Short the way your chauffeurs travel, crunching over private
    gravel
        Each from out his warm garáge.


Oh but Wendy, when the carpet yielded to my indoor pumps
    There you stood, your gold hair streaming, handsome in the
    hall-light gleaming
There you looked and there you led me off into the game of
    clumps
Then the new Victrola playing and your funny uncle saying
'Choose your partners for a fox-trot! Dance until it's *tea* o'clock!
    Come on, young 'uns, foot it featly!' Was it chance that
    paired us neatly,
        I, who loved you so completely,
You, who pressed me closely to you, hard against your party
    frock?


'Meet me when you've finished eating!' So we met and no one
    found us.
    Oh that dark and furry cupboard while the rest played hide
    and seek!
Holding hands our two hearts beating in the bedroom silence
    round us,
    Holding hands and hardly hearing sudden footstep, thud and
    shriek.
Love that lay too deep for kissing—'Where *is* Wendy? Wendy's
    missing!'
        Love so pure it *had* to end,
Love so strong that I was frighten'd when you gripped my
    fingers tight and
        Hugging, whispered 'I'm your friend.'

Good-bye Wendy! Send the fairies, pinewood elf and larch tree
    gnome,
  Spingle-spangled stars are peeping at the lush Lagonda creeping
Down the winding ways of tarmac to the leaded lights of
    home.
  There, among the silver birches, all the bells of all the
    churches
Sounded in the bath-waste running out into the frosty air.
  Wendy speeded my undressing, Wendy is the sheet's caressing
    Wendy bending gives a blessing,
Holds me as I drift to dreamland, safe inside my slumberwear.

# EDMUND BLUNDEN

## *The Recovery*

From the dark mood's control
  I free this man; there's light still in the West.
The most virtuous, chaste, melodious soul
  Never was better blest.


Here medicine for the mind
  Lies in a gilded shade; this feather stirs
And my faith lives; the touch of this tree's rind,—
  And temperate sense recurs.


No longer the loud pursuit
  Of self-made clamours dulls the ear; here dwell
Twilight societies, twig, fungus, root,
  Soundless, and speaking well.

Beneath the accustomed dome
  Of this chance-planted, many-centuried tree
The snake-marked earthy multitudes are come
  To breathe their hour like me.

The leaf comes curling down,
  Another and another, gleam on gleam;
Above, celestial leafage glistens on,
  Borne by time's blue stream.

The meadow-stream will serve
  For my refreshment; that high glory yields
Imaginings that slay; the safe paths curve
  Through unexalted fields

Like these, where now no more
  My early angels walk and call and fly,
But the mouse stays his nibbling, to explore
  My eye with his bright eye.


## Another Altar

I am Forgetfulness. I am that shadow
Of whom well warned you thought your pathway clear.
You need sharp eyes to catch such silent shadows.
Not all your wakeful plans and resolution
Outsoldiered me; you heard me at last low-laughing,
'When the steed's stolen, shut the stable-door.'
This, too, is nothing of mine. No sly ambition
Nor malice moves me; but my part is fixed
In changing onward life from scene to scene,
Necessitating futures of surprise,
Solving some enigmas, much preserving

7

To bloom a wonder in a way the sowers
Could never have guessed. I touch the cells of the mind,
And some are by that finger barred and bolted;
It may be but a moment that I triumph;
Consider what my moments still achieve.

Through me the wife learns who the mistress is,
And where. I trap the assassin, and safe murder
Becomes a dance on air. One look from me
And the mind's eye of the signalman is dimmed
And wreckage piles and flames above the dead.
I have contrived that some most secret treasures
Shall lie an age untouched, and late-discovered
Should be the source of hope and peace; I leave
The child's toy to become posterity's marvel,
From lost Tanagra; this quaint poniard lurked
Under my influence, where the culprit stowed it,
To tell man something of his martyrdoms,
Upon a day. From these my hoarded papers
At length uncovered, an impoverished fame
Grows full and noon-day clear; with that, your scholar
Is charmed with joys not his, and shall not fail
Of praise and proud remembrance—while I will.
Be sure, unsure of most, that I will make
An instrument of you this very day,
That I may weave my share of Then and Now,
A web that greater gods design—with me.
He that now writes the words I whisper to him
Has here and there unknowingly surrendered
To my caprice, if so he please to style it,
And will still find his early morning again,
Through me, after a dry and drouthy journey,
All fresh and violet-dewy; he, at least,
Will not disdain to bow to me as one,
Among the more ingenious undergods.

# *In my Time*

Touched with a certain silver light
In each man's retrospection,
There are important hours; some others
Seem to grow kingfisher's feathers,
Or glow like sunflowers; my affection
In the first kind finds more delight.


I would not challenge you to discover
Finally why you dwell
In this ward or that of your experience.
Men may vary without variance.
Each vase knows the note, the bell,
Which thrills it like a lover.


When I am silent, when a distance
Dims my response, forgive;
Accept that when the past has beckoned,
There is no help; all else comes second;
Agree, the way to live
Is not to dissect existence.


All the more waive common reason
If the passion when revealed
Seem of poor blood; if the silver hour
Be nothing but an uncouth, shot-torn tower,
And a column crossing a field,
Bowed men, to a dead horizon.

9

# Report on Experience

I have been young, and now am not too old;
And I have seen the righteous forsaken,
His health, his honour and his quality taken.
    This is not what we were formerly told.

I have seen a green country, useful to the race,
Knocked silly with guns and mines, its villages vanished,
Even the last rat and last kestrel banished—
    God bless us all, this was peculiar grace.

I knew Seraphina; Nature gave her hue,
Glance, sympathy, note, like one from Eden.
I saw her smile warp, heard her lyric deaden;
    She turned to harlotry;—this I took to be new.

Say what you will, our God sees how they run.
These disillusions are His curious proving
That He loves humanity and will go on loving;
    Over there are faith, life, virtue in the sun.


# To Our Catchment Board

Startling all spirits, dreams, and secrets
Out of the woods that verged on my first river,
The engineers arrived, large friendly men
With much tobacco armed, and drainage schemes.
They had no special hate against my river,
And indeed loved it, as a henwife loves
Some fated fowl, 'Regardez, qu'elle est belle'.
With truck and shovel, chain and claw, horse-power
Obeyed the office; hawthorns thought immortal
Found they were not, and oaks of kingliest antler
Left their old vantage over my first river.

Needs not to tell that flag and sedge and plantain
From humbler camp, but privileged, were sacked,
And snags that poked their snouts above the stream
In summer, trying to be crocodiles,
Were soon exposed ashore for what they were.
In mathematic channels reinforced
With best cement (as far as means would run)
The river took his solitary way.
Catchment as catchment can, and I'll not say
The work was wrong.
                              For I have known my river
Since this brave century opened, and have noted
A certain permanence, a personality,
A liking almost for each opposition,
A willingness to make the best of things.
And now the foreman and his squad and tackle
Have moved a few miles on, and the wilful stream
Invents new rippling-places and underminings,
Long strands and sands; by whose example moved
The willow-wood may gather, the full moon
Sow sacred oaks, and some new child in time
Find in their shadow forms of grace I found,
And by their dance and by the wavelets' chime
Be blest till sense in deeper floods be drowned.


# NORMAN CAMERON

## *Central Europe*

Despite their boastful Margraves and their flags
The inland years—fat peasants winterbound,
Stunned by the heat of their enormous stoves,
Whimpering fear of baleful gods and wolves—
Have set a bloody darkness in their souls.

Still they can see, fixed amid this red haze
Of swimming particles, the forest-faces,
Come, following the deeper shade, to town.

They need a wind bringing up gulls and salt,
Sailors and nabobs with new foreign gifts,
To blow their crannies free of ancient fear.

## Steep, Stone Steps

Steep, stone steps, stinking with washing water—
Italy inhales its incense, Dante's derelict daughter.
Poverty, Peter's Pence, politics, capital, conniving
Thieves thwart the thankless struggler's stalwart striving:
Hard, hoarding husbandry doomed, daunted, defeated;
Master masons, metalworkers chidden, checked, cheated.
Rich rogues revel, frauds fatten: what wonder
Dignity departs, patriotism perishes, petty plunder,
Servile subterfuges spread social suppuration?
Nevertheless nature's high heart carries consolation:
Generosity, joy, gentleness, mankind's measureless mines,
Love, laughter, lavishly live, sun shines.

*Naples, March* 1944

# ROY CAMPBELL

## The Zebras

From the dark woods that breathe of fallen showers,
Harnessed with level rays in golden reins,
The zebras draw the dawn across the plains
Wading knee-deep among the scarlet flowers.
The sunlight, zithering their flanks with fire,
Flashes between the shadows as they pass
Barred with electric tremors through the grass
Like wind along the gold strings of a lyre.

Into the flushed air snorting rosy plumes
That smoulder round their feet in drifting fumes,
With dove-like voices call the distant fillies,
While round the herds the stallion wheels his flight,
Engine of beauty volted with delight,
To roll his mare among the trampled lilies.


## The Zulu Girl

When in the sun the hot red acres smoulder,
Down where the sweating gang its labour plies,
A girl flings down her hoe, and from her shoulder
Unslings her child tormented by the flies.

She takes him to a ring of shadow pooled
By thorn-trees: purpled with the blood of ticks,
While her sharp nails, in slow caresses ruled,
Prowl through his hair with sharp electric clicks,

His sleepy mouth plugged by the heavy nipple,
Tugs like a puppy, grunting as he feeds:
Through his frail nerves her own deep languors ripple
Like a broad river sighing through its reeds.

Yet in that drowsy stream his flesh imbibes
An old unquenched unsmotherable heat—
The curbed ferocity of beaten tribes,
The sullen dignity of their defeat.

Her body looms above him like a hill
Within whose shade a village lies at rest,
Or the first cloud so terrible and still
That bears the coming harvest in its breast.

# On Some South African Novelists

Youd raise the firm restraint with which they write—
I'm with you there, of course:
They use the snaffle and the curb all right,
But where's the bloody horse?

## E. E. CUMMINGS

### the Cambridge ladies

the Cambridge ladies who live in furnished souls
are unbeautiful and have comfortable minds
(also, with the church's protestant blessings
daughters, unscented shapeless spirited)
they believe in Christ and Longfellow, both dead,
are invariably interested in so many things—
at the present writing one still finds
delighted fingers knitting for the is it Poles?
perhaps. While permanent faces coyly bandy
scandal of Mrs. N and Professor D
. . . the Cambridge ladies do not care, above
Cambridge if sometimes in its box of
sky lavender and cornerless, the
moon rattles like a fragment of angry candy

### what if a much of a which of a wind

what if a much of a which of a wind
gives the truth to summer's lie;
bloodies with dizzying leaves the sun
and yanks immortal stars awry?

Blow king to beggar and queen to seem
(blow friend to fiend: blow space to time)
—when skies are hanged and ocean's drowned,
the single secret will still be man

what if a keen of a lean wind flays
screaming hills with sleet and snow:
strangles valleys by ropes of thing
and stifles forests in white ago?
Blow hope to terror; blow seeing to blind
(blow pity to envy and soul to mind)
—whose hearts are mountains, roots are trees,
it's they shall cry hallo to the spring

what if a dawn of a doom of a dream
bites this universe in two,
peels for ever out of his grave
and sprinkles nowhere with me and you?
Blow soon to never and never to twice
(blow life to isn't: blow death to was)
—all nothing's only our hugest home;
the most who die, the more we live

### it's over a (see just

it's over a (see just
over this) wall
the apples are (yes
they're gravensteins) all
as red as to lose
and as round as to find.

Each why of a leaf says
(floating each how)
you're which as to die
(each green of a new)
you're who as to grow
but you're he as to do

what must (whispers) be must
be (the wise fool)
if living's to give
so breathing's to steal—
five wishes are five
and one hand is a mind

then over our thief goes
(you go and i)
has pulled (for he's we)
such fruit from what bough
that someone called they
made him pay with his now.

But over a (see just
over this) wall
the red and the round
(they're gravensteins) fall
with kind of a blind
big sound on the ground

## *you shall above all things be glad and young*

you shall above all things be glad and young.
For if you're young, whatever life you wear

it will become you; and if you are glad
whatever's living will yourself become.

Girlboys may nothing more than boygirls need:
i can entirely her only love

whose any mystery makes every man's
flesh put space on; and his mind take off time

that you should ever think, may god forbid
and (in his mercy) your true lover spare:
for that way knowledge lies, the foetal grave
called progress, and negation's dead undoom.

I'd rather learn from one bird how to sing
than teach ten thousand stars how not to dance

# W. H. DAVIES

## I am the Poet Davies, William

I am the Poet Davies, William,
    I sin without a blush or blink:
I am a man that lives to eat;
    I am a man that lives to drink.

My face is large, my lips are thick,
    My skin is coarse and black almost;
But the ugliest feature is my verse,
    Which proves my soul is black and lost.

Thank heaven thou didst not marry me,
    A poet full of blackest evil;
For how to manage my damned soul
    Will puzzle many a flaming devil.

17

# The Bust

When I was wandering far from home,
I left a woman in my room
To clean my hearth and floor, and dust
My shelves and pictures, books and bust.

When I came back a welcome glow
Burned in her eyes—her voice was low;
And everything was in its place,
As clean and bright as her own face.

But when I looked more closely there,
The dust was on my dark, bronze hair;
The nose and eyebrows too were white—
And yet the lips were clean and bright.

The years have gone, and so has she,
But still the truth remains with me—
How that hard mouth was once kept clean
By living lips that kissed unseen.


# The Tugged Hand

I have no ears or eyes
    For either bird or flower;
Music and lovely blooms
    Must bide their lighter hour;
So let them wait awhile—
    For yet another day

Till I at last forget
    The woman lying dead;
And how a lonely child
    Came to his mother's bed
And tugged at her cold hand—
    And could not make it play.

# WALTER DE LA MARE

## *The Bead Mat*

We had climbed the last steep flight of stairs;
   Alone were she and I:
'It's something I wanted to give to you,'
   She whispered with a sigh.

There, in her own small room she stood—
   Where the last beam of sun
Burned in the glass—and showed me what
   For me she had done:—

An oblong shining mat of beads,
   Yellow and white and green,
And where the dark-blue middle was
   A gold between.

I heard no far-off voice, no sound:
   Only her clear grey eyes
Drank in the thoughts that in my face
   Passed shadow-wise.

She clasped her hands, and turned her head,
   And in the watchful glass
She saw how many things had seen
   All that had passed.

She snatched her gift away: her cheek
   With scarlet was aflame:
'It isn't *anything*,' she said,
   'If *we*'re the same!'

Her eyes were like a stormy sea,
  Forlorn, and vast, and grey;
Wherein a little beaten ship
  Flew through the spray.


## The Feckless Dinner Party

'Who are we waiting for?' '*Soup* burnt?' . . . Eight—
  'Only the tiniest party.—Us!'
'Darling! Divine!' 'Ten minutes late—'
  'And my digest—' 'I'm *ra*venous!'


' "Toomes"?'—'Oh, he's new.' 'Looks crazed, I guess.'
  ' "Married"—*Again!*' 'Well; more or less!'


'Dinner is *served*!' ' "Dinner is served"!'
  'Is served?' 'Is served.' 'Ah, yes.'


'Dear Mr. Prout, will you take down
  The Lilith in leaf-green by the fire?
Blanche Ogleton? . . .' 'How coy a frown!—
  Hasn't she borrowed *Eve's* attire?'
'Morose Old Adam!' 'Charmed—I vow.'
  'Come then, and meet her now.'


'Now, Dr. Mallus—would you please?—
  Our daring poetess, Delia Seek?'
'The lady with the bony knees?'
  'And—*entre nous*—less song than beak.'
'Sharing her past with Simple Si.'
  '*Bare* facts! He'll blush!' 'Oh, fie!'

20

'And *you*, Sir Nathan—false but fair!—
  That fountain of wit, Aurora Pert.'
'More wit than It, poor dear! But there . . .'
  'Pitiless Pasha! *And* such a flirt!'
' "Flirt"! *Me?*' 'Who else?' 'You here. . . . Who can . . . ?'
  'In*corr*igible man!'


'And now, Mr. Simon—little me!—
  Last and—' 'By no means least!' 'Oh, come!
What naughty, naughty flattery!
  *Honey!*—I *hear* the creature hum!'
'Sweets for the sweet, *I* always say!'
  ' "Always"? . . . We're last.' '*This* way?' . . .


'No, sir; straight on, please.' 'I'd have vowed!—
  I came the other . . .' 'It's queer; I'm sure . . .'
'What frightful pictures!' 'Fiends!' 'The *crowd*!'
  'Such news!' 'I can't endure . . .'


'Yes, *there* they go.' 'Heavens! *Are* we right?'
  'Follow up closer!' ' "Prout"?—sand-blind!'
'This endless . . .' 'Who's turned down the light?'
  'Keep calm! They're close behind.'


'Oh! Dr. Mallus; what dismal stairs!'
  'I hate these old Victor . . .' 'Dry rot!'
'Darker and darker!' 'Fog!' 'The air's . . .'
  'Scarce breathable!' 'Hell!' '*What?*'


'The banister's gone!' 'It's deep; keep close!'
  'We're going down and down!' 'What fun!'
'Damp! Why, my shoes . . .' 'It's slimy. . . . Not *moss*!'
  'I'm freezing cold!' 'Let's run.'

' . . . Behind us. I'm giddy. . . .' 'The catacombs . . .'
    'That shout!' 'Who's there?' 'I'm *alone*!' 'Stand back!'
'She said, Lead . . .' 'Oh!' 'Where's Toomes?' '*Toomes*!'
    'TOOMES!'
    'Stifling!' 'My skull will crack!'

'Sir Nathan! *Ai!*' 'I *say*! Toomes! Prout!'
    'Where? Where?' ' "Our silks and fine array" . . .'
'She's mad.' 'I'm dying!' 'Oh, let me *out*!'
    'My God! We've lost our way!' . . .

And now how sad-serene the abandoned house,
Whereon at dawn the spring-tide sunbeams beat;
And time's slow pace alone is ominous,
And naught but shadows of noonday therein meet;
Domestic microcosm, only a Trump could rouse:
And, pondering darkly, in the silent rooms,
He who misled them all—the butler, Toomes.


## EMILY DICKINSON

### *I Taste a Liquor Never Brewed*

I taste a liquor never brewed,
From tankards scooped in pearl;
Not all the vats upon the Rhine
Yield such an alcohol!

Inebriate of air am I,
And debauchee of dew,
Reeling, through endless summer days,
From inns of molten blue.

When landlords turn the drunken bee
Out of the foxglove's door,
When butterflies renounce their drams,
I shall but drink the more!

Till seraphs swing their snowy hats,
And saints to windows run,
To see the little tippler
Leaning against the sun!


## Faith is a Fine Invention

Faith is a fine invention
For gentlemen who see;
But microscopes are prudent
In an emergency!


## The Sky is Low, the Clouds are Mean

The sky is low, the clouds are mean,
A travelling flake of snow
Across a barn or through a rut
Debates if it will go.

A narrow wind complains all day
How some one treated him;
Nature, like us, is sometimes caught
Without her diadem.

# I Heard a Fly Buzz when I Died

I heard a fly buzz when I died;
The stillness in the room
Was like the stillness in the air
Between the heaves of storm.

The eyes around had wrung them dry,
And breaths were gathering firm
For that last onset, when the king
Be witnessed in the room.

I willed my keepsakes, signed away
What portion of me be
Assignable—and then it was
There interposed a fly,

With blue, uncertain, stumbling buzz,
Between the light and me;
And then the windows failed, and then
I could not see to see.

# A Narrow Fellow in the Grass

A narrow fellow in the grass
Occasionally rides;
You may have met him,—did you not?
His notice sudden is.

The grass divides as with a comb,
A spotted shaft is seen;
And then it closes at your feet
And opens further on.

He likes a boggy acre,
A floor too cool for corn.
Yet when a child, and barefoot,
I more than once, at morn,

Have passed, I thought, a whip-lash
Unbraiding in the sun,—
When, stooping to secure it,
It wrinkled, and was gone.

Several of nature's people
I know, and they know me;
I feel for them a transport
Of cordiality;

But never met this fellow,
Attended or alone,
Without a tighter breathing,
And zero at the bone.


# T. S. ELIOT

## The Love Song of J. Alfred Prufrock

*S'io credesse che mia risposta fosse*
*A persona che mai tornasse al mondo,*
*Questa fiamma staria senza piu scosse.*
*Ma perciocche giammai di questo fondo*
*Non tòrno vivo alcun, s'i'odo il vero,*
*Senza tema d'infamia ti rispondo.*

Let us go then, you and I,
When the evening is spread out against the sky
Like a patient etherised upon a table;

Let us go, through certain half-deserted streets,
The muttering retreats
Of restless nights in one-night cheap hotels
And sawdust restaurants with oyster-shells:
Streets that follow like a tedious argument
Of insidious intent
To lead you to an overwhelming question. . . .
Oh, do not ask, 'What is it?'
Let us go and make our visit.

In the room the women come and go
Talking of Michelangelo.
The yellow fog that rubs its back upon the window-panes,
The yellow smoke that rubs its muzzle on the window-panes
Licked its tongue into the corners of the evening,
Lingered upon the pools that stand in drains,
Let fall upon its back the soot that falls from chimneys,
Slipped by the terrace, made a sudden leap,
And seeing that it was a soft October night,
Curled once about the house, and fell asleep.

And indeed there will be time
For the yellow smoke that slides along the street,
Rubbing its back upon the window-panes;
There will be time, there will be time
To prepare a face to meet the faces that you meet;
There will be time to murder and create,
And time for all the works and days of hands
That lift and drop a question on your plate;
Time for you and time for me,
And time yet for a hundred indecisions,
And for a hundred visions and revisions,
Before the taking of a toast and tea.
In the room the women come and go
Talking of Michelangelo.

And indeed there will be time
To wonder, 'Do I dare?' and 'Do I dare?'
Time to turn back and descend the stair,
With a bald spot in the middle of my hair—
(They will say: 'How his hair is growing thin!')
My morning coat, my collar mounting firmly to the chin,
My necktie rich and modest, but asserted by a simple pin—
(They will say: 'But how his arms and legs are thin!')
Do I dare
Disturb the universe?
In a minute there is time
For decisions and revisions which a minute will reverse.


For I have known them all already, known them all:
Have known the evenings, mornings, afternoons,
I have measured out my life with coffee spoons;
I know the voices dying with a dying fall
Beneath the music from a farther room.
    So how should I presume?


And I have known the eyes already, known them all—
The eyes that fix you in a formulated phrase,
And when I am formulated, sprawling on a pin,
When I am pinned and wriggling on the wall,
Then how should I begin
To spit out all the butt-ends of my days and ways?
    And how should I presume?


And I have known the arms already, known them all—
Arms that are braceleted and white and bare
(But in the lamplight, downed with light brown hair!)
Is it perfume from a dress
That makes me so digress?

27

Arms that lie along a table, or wrap about a shawl.
   And should I then presume?
   And how should I begin?

     .     .     .     .     .     .     .

Shall I say, I have gone at dusk through narrow streets
And watched the smoke that rises from the pipes
Of lonely men in shirt-sleeves, leaning out of windows? . . .
I should have been a pair of ragged claws
Scuttling across the floors of silent seas.

     .     .     .     .     .     .

And the afternoon, the evening sleeps so peacefully!
Smoothed by long fingers,
Asleep . . . tired . . . or it malingers,
Stretched on the floor, here beside you and me.
Should I, after tea and cakes and ices,
Have the strength to force the moment to its crisis?
But though I have wept and fasted, wept and prayed,
Though I have seen my head (grown slightly bald) brought in
    upon a platter,
I am no prophet—and here's no great matter;
I have seen the moment of my greatness flicker,
And I have seen the eternal Footman hold my coat, and snicker,
And in short, I was afraid.

And would it have been worth it, after all
After the cups, the marmalade, the tea,
Among the porcelain, among some talk of you and me,
Would it have been worth while,
To have bitten off the matter with a smile,
To have squeezed the Universe into a ball,
To roll it toward some overwhelming question,
To say: 'I am Lazarus, come from the dead,
Come back to tell you all, I shall tell you all'—
If one, settling a pillow by her head,
   Should say: 'That is not what I meant at all;
   That is not it, at all.'

And would it have been worth it after all,
Would it have been worth while,
After the sunsets and the dooryards and the sprinkled streets,
After the novels, after the teacups, after the skirts that trail along
     the floor—
And this, and so much more?—
It is impossible to say just what I mean!
But as if a magic lantern threw the nerves in patterns on a screen:
Would it have been worth while
If one, settling a pillow or throwing off a shawl,
And turning toward the window, should say:
   'That is not it at all,
   That is not what I meant, at all.'

        .        .        .        .        .        .        .

No! I am not Prince Hamlet, nor was meant to be;
Am an attendant lord, one that will do
To swell a progress, start a scene or two,
Advise the prince; no doubt, an easy tool,
Deferential, glad to be of use,
Politic, cautious, and meticulous;
Full of high sentence, but a bit obtuse;
At times, indeed, almost ridiculous—
Almost, at times, the Fool.

I grow old . . . I grow old . . .
I shall wear the bottoms of my trousers rolled.

Shall I part my hair behind? Do I dare to eat a peach?
I shall wear white flannel trousers, and walk upon the beach.
I have heard the mermaids singing, each to each.

I do not think that they will sing to me.

I have seen them riding seaward on the waves
Combing the white hair of the waves blown back
When the wind blows the water white and black.

We have lingered in the chambers of the sea
By sea-girls wreathed with seaweed red and brown
Till human voices wake us, and we drown.


## Animula

*(The little soul)*

'Issues from the hand of God, the simple soul'
To a flat world of changing lights and noise,
To light, dark, dry or damp, chilly or warm;
Moving between the legs of tables and of chairs,
Rising or falling, grasping at kisses and toys,
Advancing boldly, sudden to take alarm,
Retreating to the corner of arm and knee,
Eager to be reassured, taking pleasure
In the fragrant brilliance of the Christmas tree,
Pleasure in the wind, the sunlight and the sea;
Studies the sunlit pattern on the floor
And running stags around a silver tray;
Confounds the actual and the fanciful,
Content with playing-cards and kings and queens,
What the fairies do and what the servants say.
The heavy burden of the growing soul
Perplexes and offends more, day by day;
Week by week, offends and perplexes more
With the imperatives of 'is and seems'
And may and may not, desire and control.
The pain of living and the drug of dreams
Curl up the small soul in the window seat
Behind the *Encyclopaedia Britannica*.

Issues from the hand of time the simple soul
Irresolute and selfish, misshapen, lame,
Unable to fare forward or retreat,
Fearing the warm reality, the offered good,
Denying the importunity of the blood,
Shadow of its own shadows, spectre in its own gloom,
Leaving disordered papers in a dusty room;
Living first in the silence after the viaticum.

Pray for Guiterriez, avid of speed and power,
For Boudin, blown to pieces,
For this one who made a great fortune,
And that one who went his own way.
Pray for Floret, by the boarhound slain between the yew trees,
Pray for us now and at the hour of our birth.


## Lines for an Old Man

The tiger in the tiger-pit
Is not more irritable than I.
The whipping tail is not more still
Than when I smell the enemy
Writhing in the essential blood
Or dangling from the friendly tree.
When I lay bare the tooth of wit
The hissing over the archèd tongue
Is more affectionate than hate,
More bitter than the love of youth,
And inaccessible by the young.
Reflected from my golden eye
The dullard knows that he is mad.
Tell me if I am not glad!

# WILLIAM EMPSON

## *To an Old Lady*

Ripeness is all; her in her cooling planet
Revere; do not presume to think her wasted.
Project her no projectile, plan nor man it;
Gods cool in turn, by the sun long outlasted.

Our earth alone given no name of god *like planets*
Gives, too, no hold for such a leap to aid her;
Landing, you break some palace and seem odd;
Bees sting their need, the keeper's queen invader.

No, to your telescope; spy out the land;
Watch while her ritual is still to see,
Still stand her temples emptying in the sand
Whose waves o'erthrew their crumbled tracery;

Still stand uncalled-on her soul's appanage;
Much social detail whose successor fades,
Wit used to run a house and to play Bridge,
And tragic fervour, to dismiss her maids.

Years her precession do not throw from gear.
She reads a compass certain of her pole;
Confident, finds no confines on her sphere,
Whose failing crops are in her sole control.

Stars how much further from me fill my night,
Strange that she too should be inaccessible,
Who shares my sun. He curtains her from sight,
And but in darkness is she visible.

# D. J. ENRIGHT

## *University Examinations in Egypt*

The air is thick with nerves and smoke: pens tremble in sweating
    hands:
Domestic police flit in and out, with smelling salts and aspirin:
And servants, grave-faced but dirty, pace the aisles,
With coffee, Player's and coca-cola.


Was it like this in my day, at my place? Memory boggles
Between the aggressive fly and curious ant—but did I really
Pause in my painful flight to light a cigarette or swallow drugs?


The nervous eye, patrolling these hot unhappy victims,
Flinches at the symptoms of a year's hard teaching—
'Falstaff indulged in drinking and sexcess', and then,
'Doolittle was a dusty man' and 'Dr. Johnson edited the Yellow
    Book.'


Culture and aspirin: the urgent diploma, the straining brain—all
    in the evening fall
To tric-trac in the café, to Hollywood in the picture-house:
Behind, like tourist posters, the glamour of laws and committees,
Wars for freedom, cheat text-books, national aspirations—
And, farther still and very faint, the foreign ghost of happy
    Shakespeare,
Keats who really loved things, Akhenaton who adored the
    Sun,
And Goethe who never thought of Thought.

# JAMES ELROY FLECKER

## *To a Poet a Thousand Years Hence*

I who am dead a thousand years,
    And wrote this sweet archaic song,
Send you my words for messengers
    The way I shall not pass along.

I care not if you bridge the seas,
    Or ride secure the cruel sky,
Or build consummate palaces
    Of metal or of masonry.

But have you wine and music still,
    And statues and a bright-eyed love,
And foolish thoughts of good and ill,
    And prayers to them who sit above?

How shall we conquer? Like a wind
    That falls at eve our fancies blow,
And old Maeonides the blind
    Said it three thousand years ago.

O friend unseen, unborn, unknown,
    Student of our sweet English tongue,
Read out my words at night, alone:
    I was a poet, I was young.

Since I can never see your face,
    And never shake you by the hand,
I send my soul through time and space
    To greet you. You will understand.

# ROBERT FROST

## *The Tuft of Flowers*

I went to turn the grass once after one
Who mowed it in the dew before the sun.

The dew was gone that made his blade so keen
Before I came to view the levelled scene.

I looked for him behind an isle of trees;
I listened for his whetstone on the breeze.

But he had gone his way, the grass all mown,
And I must be, as he had been,—alone.

'As all must be,' I said within my heart,
'Whether they work together or apart.'

But as I said it, swift there passed me by
On noiseless wing a bewildered butterfly,

Seeking with memories grown dim o'er night
Some resting flower of yesterday's delight.

And once I marked his flight go round and round,
As where some flower lay withering on the ground.

And then he flew as far as eye could see,
And then on tremulous wing came back to me.

I thought of questions that had no reply,
And would have turned to toss the grass to dry;

But he turned first, and led my eye to look
At a tall tuft of flowers beside a brook,

A leaping tongue of bloom the scythe had spared
Beside a reedy brook the scythe had bared.

The mower in the dew had loved them thus
By leaving them to flourish, not for us,

Nor yet to draw one thought of ours to him,
But from sheer morning gladness at the brim.

The butterfly and I had lit upon,
Nevertheless, a message from the dawn,

That made me hear the wakening birds around,
And hear his long scythe whispering to the ground,

And feel a spirit kindred to my own;
So that henceforth I worked no more alone;

But glad with him, I worked as with his aid,
And weary, sought at noon with him the shade;

And dreaming, as it were, held brotherly speech
With one whose thought I had not hoped to reach.

'Men work together,' I told him from the heart,
'Whether they work together or apart.'

# Mending Wall

Something there is that doesn't love a wall,
That sends the frozen-ground-swell under it,
And spills the upper boulders in the sun;
And makes gaps even two can pass abreast.
The work of hunters is another thing:
I have come after them and made repair
Where they have left not one stone on a stone,
But they would have the rabbit out of hiding,
To please the yelping dogs. The gaps I mean,
No one has seen them made or heard them made,
But at spring mending-time we find them there.
I let my neighbour know beyond the hill;
And on a day we meet to walk the line
And set the wall between us once again.
We keep the wall between us as we go.
To each the boulders that have fallen to each.
And some are loaves and some so nearly balls
We have to use a spell to make them balance:
'Stay where you are until our backs are turned!'
We wear our fingers rough with handling them.
Oh, just another kind of outdoor game,
One on a side. It comes to little more:
There where it is we do not need the wall:
He is all pine and I am apple orchard.
My apple trees will never get across
And eat the cones under his pines, I tell him.
He only says, 'Good fences make good neighbours.'
Spring is the mischief in me, and I wonder
If I could put a notion in his head:
'*Why* do they make good neighbours? Isn't it
Where there are cows? But here there are no cows.
Before I built a wall I'd ask to know
What I was walling in or walling out,

And to whom I was like to give offence.
Something there is that doesn't love a wall,
That wants it down.' I could say 'Elves' to him,
But it's not elves exactly, and I'd rather
He said it for himself. I see him there
Bringing a stone grasped firmly by the top
In each hand, like an old-stone savage armed.
He moves in darkness as it seems to me,
Not of woods only and the shade of trees.
He will not go behind his father's saying,
And he likes having thought of it so well
He says again, 'Good fences make good neighbours.'

## Too Anxious for Rivers

Look down the long valley and there stands a mountain
That someone has said is the end of the world.
Then what of this river that having arisen
Must find where to pour itself into and empty?
I never saw so much swift water run cloudless.
Oh, I have been often too anxious for rivers
To leave it to them to get out of their valleys.
The truth is the river flows into the canyon
Of Ceasing to Question What Doesn't Concern Us,
As sooner or later we have to cease somewhere.
No place to get lost like too far in the distance.
It may be a mercy the dark closes round us
So broodingly soon in every direction.
The world as we know is an elephant's howdah;
The elephant stands on the back of a turtle;
The turtle in turn on a rock in the ocean.
And how much longer a story has science
Before she must put out the light on the children
And tell them the rest of the story is dreaming?

'You children may dream it and tell it tomorrow.'
Time was we were molten, time was we were vapour.
What set us on fire and what set us revolving
Lucretius the Epicurean might tell us
'Twas something we knew all about to begin with
And needn't have fared into space like his master
To find 'twas the effort, the essay of love.

# DAVID GASCOYNE

## *Snow in Europe*

Out of their slumber Europeans spun
Dense dreams: appeasement, miracle, glimpsed flash
Of a new golden era; but could not restrain
The vertical white weight that fell last night
And made their continent a blank.

Hush, says the sameness of the snow
The Ural and the Jura now rejoin
The furthest Arctic's desolation. All is one
Sheer monotone: plain, mountain; country, town:
Contours and boundaries no longer show.

The warring flags hang colourless awhile;
Now midnight's icy zero feigns a truce
Between the signs and seasons, and fades out
All shots and cries. But when the great thaw comes,
How red shall be the melting snow, how loud the drums!

*Christmas* 1938

# ROBERT GRAVES

## *Lost Acres*

These acres, always again lost
  By every new ordnance-survey
And searched for at exhausting cost
  Of time and thought, are still away.

They have their paper-substitute—
  Intercalation of an inch
At the so-many-thousandth foot:
  And no one parish feels the pinch.

But lost they are, despite all care,
  And perhaps are likely to be bound
Together in a piece somewhere,
  A plot of undiscovered ground.

Invisible, they have the spite
  To swerve the tautest measuring-chain
And the exact theodolite
  Perched every side of them in vain.

Yet, be assured, we have no need
  To plot such acres of the mind
With prehistoric fern and reed
  And monsters such as heroes find.

Maybe they have their flowers, their birds,
  Their trees behind the phantom fence,
But of a substance without words:
  To walk there would be loss of sense.

# On Dwelling

Courtesies of good-morning and good-evening
From rustic lips fail as the town encroaches:
Soon nothing passes but the cold quick stare
Of eyes that see ghosts, yet too many for fear.

Here I too walk, silent myself in wonder
At a town not mine yet plainly co-extensive
With mine, even in days coincident:
In mine I dwell, in theirs like them I haunt.

And the green country, should I turn again there?
My bumpkin neighbours loom even ghostlier:
Like trees they murmur or like blackbirds sing
Courtesies of good-morning and good-evening.

# The Poets

Any honest housewife would sort them out,
Having a nose for fish, an eye for apples.
Is it any mystery who are the sound,
And who the rotten? Never, by her lights.

Any honest housewife who, by ill-fortune,
Ever engaged a slut to scrub for her
Could instantly distinguish from the workers
The lazy, liars and the petty thieves.

Does this denote a sixth peculiar sense   Chastity
Gifted to housewives for their vestal needs?
Or is it failure of the usual five
In all unthrifty writers on this head?

# The Great-grandmother

That aged woman with the bass voice
And yellowing white hair: believe her.
Though to your grandfather, her son, she lied
And to your father disingenuously
Told half the tale as the whole,
Yet she was honest with herself,
Knew disclosure was not yet due,
Knows it is due now.


She will conceal nothing of consequence
From you, her great-grandchildren
(So distant the relationship,
So near her term),
Will tell you frankly, she has waited
Only for your sincere indifference
To exorcize that filial regard
Which has estranged her, seventy years,
From the folk of her house.


Confessions of old distaste
For music, sighs and roses—
Their false-innocence assaulting her,
Breaching her hard heart;
Of the pleasures of a full purse,
Of clean brass and clean linen,
Of being alone at last;
Disgust with the ailing poor
To whom she was bountiful;
How the prattle of young children
Vexed more than if they whined;
How she preferred cats.

She will say, yes, she acted well,
Took such pride in the art
That none of them suspected, even,
Her wrathful irony
In doing what they asked
Better than they could ask it. . . .
But, ah, how grudgingly her will returned
After the severance of each navel-cord,
And fled how far again,
When again she was kind!

She has outlasted all man-uses,
As was her first resolve:
Happy and idle like a port
After the sea's recession,
She does not misconceive the nature
Of shipmen or of ships.
Hear her, therefore, as the latest voice;
The intervening generations (drifting
On tides of fancy still), ignore.

## Lollocks   petty annoyances

By sloth on sorrow fathered,
These dusty-featured Lollocks
Have their nativity in all disordered
Backs of cupboard drawers.

They play hide and seek
Among collars and novels
And empty medicine bottles

And letters from abroad
That will never be answered.

Every sultry night
They plague little children,
Gurgling from the cistern,
Humming from the air,
Skewing up the bed-clothes,
Twitching the blind.

When the imbecile agèd
Are over-long in dying
And the nurse drowses,
Lollocks come skipping
Up the tattered stairs
And are nasty together
In the bed's shadow.

The signs of their presence
Are boils on the neck,
Dreams of vexation suddenly recalled
In the middle of the morning,
Languor after food.
Men cannot see them,
Men cannot hear them,
Do not believe in them—
But suffer the more,
Both in neck and belly.

Women can see them—
O those naughty wives
Who sit by the fireside
Munching bread and honey,

Watching them in mischief
From corners of their eyes,
Slyly allowing them to lick
Honey-sticky fingers.

Sovereign against Lollocks
Are hard broom and soft broom,
To well comb the hair,
To well brush the shoe,
And to pay every debt
So soon as it's due.

# THOMAS HARDY (not so modern)

*b. 1840,*
*died 1928*

## *I Look into my Glass*

*work of art with form.*

*mind young*
*body old*

*loving but*
*unloved*

I look into my glass,
And view my wasting skin,
And say, 'Would God it came to pass
My heart had shrunk as thin!'

*About age.*

*melancholy &*
*regretful*
*reflection*

*Yeats greets old*
*age joyously!*

For then, I, undistrest
By hearts grown cold to me,
Could lonely wait my endless rest
With equanimity.

*of mind*

*sounds & rhythm*

*poem could have ended here, but reinforced with 3rd v*

But Time, to make me grieve,
Part steals, lets part abide;
And shakes this fragile frame at eve
With throbbings of noontide. — *stressing different - only 1*
*strong & 1 weak stress.*

45

# At a Lunar Eclipse *Philosophic,*

Thy shadow, Earth, from Pole to Central Sea,
Now steals along upon the Moon's meek shine
In even monochrome and curving line
Of imperturbable serenity.

How shall I link such sun-cast symmetry
With the torn troubled form I know as thine,
That profile, placid as a brow divine,
With continents of moil and misery?

And can immense Mortality but throw
So small a shade, and Heaven's high human scheme
Be hemmed within the coasts yon arc implies?

Is such the stellar gauge of earthly show,
Nation at war with nation, brains that teem,
Heroes, and women fairer than the skies?

# A Broken Appointment *dramatic lyric analysing, ironic*

You did not come,
And marching Time drew on, and wore me numb.—
Yet less for loss of your dear presence there
Than that I thus found lacking in your make
The high compassion which can overbear
Reluctance for pure lovingkindness' sake
Grieved I, when, as the hope-hour stroked its sum,
You did not come.

You love not me,
And love alone can lend you loyalty;
—I know and knew it. But, unto the store
Of human deeds divine in all but name,
Was it not worth a little hour or more
To add yet this: Once you, a woman, came
To soothe a time-torn man; even though it be
You love not me?


## The Self-unseeing

Here is the ancient floor,
Footworn and hollowed and thin,
Here was the former door
Where the dead feet walked in.

She sat here in her chair,
Smiling into the fire;
He who played stood there,
Bowing it higher and higher.

Childlike, I danced in a dream;
Blessings emblazoned that day;
Everything glowed with a gleam;
Yet we were looking away! ✗ unawareness


## The House of Hospitalities

Here we broached the Christmas barrel,
    Pushed up the charred log-ends;
Here we sang the Christmas carol,
    And called in friends.

Time has tired me since we met here
    When the folk now dead were young,
Since the viands were outset here
        And quaint songs sung.

And the worm has bored the viol
    That used to lead the tune,
Rust eaten out the dial
        That struck night's noon.

Now no Christmas brings in neighbours,
    And the New Year comes unlit;
Where we sang the mole now labours,
        And spiders knit.

Yet at midnight if here walking,
    When the moon sheets wall and tree,
I see forms of old time talking,
        Who smile on me.

*After a Journey*  Rhythm of dance time in regular

Hereto I come to view a voiceless ghost;
    Whither, O whither will its whim now draw me?
Up the cliff, down, till I'm lonely, lost,
    And the unseen waters' ejaculations awe me.

Where you will next be there's no knowing,
    Facing round about me everywhere,
        With your nut-coloured hair,
And gray eyes, and rose-flush coming and going.


Yes: I have re-entered your olden haunts at last;
    Through the years, through the dead scenes I have tracked
        you;
What have you now found to say of our past—
    Scanned across the dark space wherein I have lacked you?
Summer gave us sweets, but autumn wrought division?
    Things were not lastly as firstly well
        With us twain, you tell?
But all's closed now, despite Time's derision.


I see what you are doing: you are leading me on
    To the spots we knew when we haunted here together,
The waterfall, above which the mist-bow shone
    At the then fair hour in the then fair weather,
And the cave just under, with a voice still so hollow
    That it seems to call out to me from forty years ago,
        When you were all aglow,
And not the thin ghost that I now frailly follow!


Ignorant of what there is flitting here to see,
    The waked birds preen and the seals flop lazily,
Soon you will have, Dear, to vanish from me,
    For the stars close their shutters and the dawn whitens
        hazily.
Trust me, I mind not, though Life lours,
    The bringing me here; nay, bring me here again!
        I am just the same as when
Our days were a joy, and our paths through flowers.

## Where the Picnic Was

Where we made the fire
In the summer time
Of branch and briar
On the hill to the sea,
I slowly climb
Through winter mire,
And scan and trace
The forsaken place
Quite readily.

Now a cold wind blows,
And the grass is gray,
But the spot still shows
As a burnt circle—aye,
And stick-ends, charred,
Still strew the sward
Whereon I stand,
Last relic of the band
Who came that day!

Yes, I am here
Just as last year,
And the sea breathes brine
From its strange straight line
Up hither, the same
As when we four came.
—But two have wandered far
From this grassy rise
Into urban roar
Where no picnics are,
And one—has shut her eyes
For evermore.

# Heredity

*Despair of materialist*

I am the family face;
Flesh perishes, I live on,
Projecting trait and trace
Through time to times anon,
And leaping from place to place
Over oblivion.

The years-heired feature that can
In curve and voice and eye
Despise the human span
Of durance—that is I;
The eternal thing in man,
That heeds no call to die.

# JOHN HEATH-STUBBS

## Don Juan Muses

*over the dead body of the Commendador*

How beautiful, white and hard, are the teeth of this dead man—
The cold eyes fixed, and about the rigid mouth
The wrinkled lines of pain, like mountain canyons.
I have looked often upon the faces of the Dead,
And seen them carried with naked feet—bodies that once had
    been
Beautiful, obscure and draped in a plain coarse habit,
The stiff impersonal lines of Francis or Dominic—
To the cells of the grave, that always silent college.

And I remember the Day of the Dead; the offerings
Of flowers and fruit, and cakes set at their doors
By the country people, the hooded figures chanting,
And the many lights moving at noon in the sunlit square.

And now in the dark room, in the pause before
The blood is wiped from the blade, before the outcry
Begins, of the servants, and the woman's animal sobbing,
Before the scuffle in the street and the get-away,
I gaze on his cold face, where my own pride's image
Stares back at me—paternal body, stiff,
As though already he were turning to stone—
And so I wonder if this thing was not always
That which I most desired—oh, through the nights,
Those silver nights under a moon of summer,
When I carved my lust into song, or hid my face
In the dark forest of a woman's hair, or sought the comfort
And softness of their flesh; for pain deep-stemmed
Within the narrow, tension of the sinew,
Shall get no final comforting, until
I feel my living hand in a stone hand's clasp,
A stone man's eyes reflect my arrogance.


# GERARD MANLEY HOPKINS *[not so modern*

## *The Starlight Night*

Look at the stars! look, look up at the skies!
   O look at all the fire-folk sitting in the air!
   The bright boroughs, the circle-citadels there!
Down in dim woods the diamond delves! the elves'-eyes!

The grey lawns cold where gold, where quickgold lies!
  Wind-beat whitebeam! airy abeles set on a flare!
  Flake-doves sent floating forth at a farmyard scare!—
Ah well! it is all a purchase, all is a prize.

Buy then! bid then!—What?—Prayer, patience, alms, vows.
Look, look: a May-mess, like on orchard boughs!
  Look! March-bloom, like on mealed-with-yellow sallows!
These are indeed the barn; withindoors house
The shocks. This piece-bright paling shuts the spouse
  Christ home, Christ and his mother and all his hallows.


## The Windhover

### To Christ our Lord

I caught this morning morning's minion, kingdom of daylight's
        dauphin, dapple-dawn-drawn Falcon, in his riding
  Of the rolling level underneath him steady air, and striding
High there, how he rung upon the rein of a wimpling wing
In his ecstasy! then off, off forth on a swing,
  As a skate's heel sweeps smooth on a bow-bend: the hurl and
        gliding
  Rebuffed the big wind. My heart in hiding
Stirred for a bird,—the achieve of, the mastery of the thing!

Brute beauty and valour and act, oh, air, pride, plume here
  Buckle! AND the fire that breaks from thee then, a billion
Times told lovelier, more dangerous, O my chevalier!

No wonder of it: sheer plod makes plough down sillion
Shine and blue-bleak embers, ah my dear,
Fall, gall themselves, and gash gold-vermilion.

# I Wake and Feel the Fell of Dark

*Agony of soul*

I wake and feel the fell of dark, not day.   *fell = animal skin*
What hours, O what black hours we have spent
This night! what sights you, heart, saw; ways you went!
And more, in yet longer light's delay.

With witness I speak this. But where I say
Hours I mean years, mean life. And my lament
Is cries countless, cries like dead letters sent
To dearest him that lives alas! away.

*cry receives no reply*

I am gall, I am heartburn. God's most deep decree
Bitter would have me taste: my taste was me;   *sick of himself*
Bones built in me, flesh filled, blood brimmed the curse
Selfyeast of spirit a dull dough sours. I see
The lost are like this, and their scourge to be
As I am mine, their sweating selves; but worse.

## A. E. HOUSMAN *(not so modern)*

*Ballad forms 8-6-8-6 + adaptions*

### Her strong enchantments failing

*Feminine endings - down*

Her strong enchantments failing,
  Her towers of fear in wreck,
Her limbecks dried of poisons
  And the knife at her neck,

The Queen of air and darkness
  Begins to shrill and cry,
'O young man, O my slayer,
  To-morrow you shall die.'

*Poems / all country backgrounds / all concerned with being young, growing old & dying / & music & / more emotional than intellectual / craftsmanship*

O Queen of air and darkness,
  I think 'tis truth you say,
And I shall die to-morrow;
  But you will die to-day.

## When first my way to fair I took

When first my way to fair I took
  Few pence in purse had I,
And long I used to stand and look
  At things I could not buy.

Now times are altered: if I care
  To buy a thing, I can;
The pence are here and here's the fair,
  But where's the lost young man?

—To think that two and two are four
  And neither five nor three
The heart of man has long been sore
  And long 'tis like to be.

## Tell me not here, it needs not saying

Tell me not here, it needs not saying,
  What tune the enchantress plays
In aftermaths of soft September
  Or under blanching mays,
For she and I were long acquainted
  And I knew all her ways.

On russet floors, by waters idle,
  The pine lets fall its cone;
The cuckoo shouts all day at nothing
  In leafy dells alone;

And traveller's joy beguiles in autumn
   Hearts that have lost their own.

On acres of the seeded grasses
   The changing burnish heaves;
Or marshalled under moons of harvest
   Stand still all night the sheaves;
Or beeches strip in storms for winter
   And stain the wind with leaves.

Possess, as I possessed a season,
   The countries I resign,
Where over elmy plains the highway
   Would mount the hills and shine,
And full of shade the pillared forest
   Would murmur and be mine.

For nature, heartless, witless nature,
   Will neither care nor know
What stranger's feet may find the meadow
   And trespass there and go,
Nor ask amid the dews of morning
   If they are mine or no.

## Fancy's Knell

When lads were home from labour
   At Abdon under Clee,
A man would call his neighbour
   And both would send for me.
And where the light in lances
   Across the mead was laid,
There to the dances
   I fetched my flute and played.

Ours were idle pleasures,
    Yet oh, content we were,
The young to wind the measures,
    The old to heed the air;
And I to lift with playing
    From tree and tower and steep
The light delaying,
    And flute the sun to sleep.

The youth toward his fancy
    Would turn his brow of tan,
And Tom would pair with Nancy
    And Dick step off with Fan;
The girl would lift her glances
    To his, and both be mute:
Well went the dances
    At evening to the flute.

Wenlock Edge was umbered,
    And bright was Abdon Burf,
And warm between them slumbered
    The smooth green miles of turf;
Until from grass and clover
    The upshot beam would fade,
And England over
    Advanced the lofty shade.

The lofty shade advances,
    I fetch my flute and play:
Come, lads, and learn the dances
    And praise the tune to-day.
To-morrow, more's the pity,
    Away we both must hie,
To air the ditty,
    And to earth I.

# ELIZABETH JENNINGS

## *The Enemies*

Last night they came across the river and
Entered the city. Women were awake
With lights and food. They entertained the band,
Not asking what the men had come to take
Or what strange tongue they spoke
Or why they came so suddenly through the land.


Now in the morning all the town is filled
With stories of the swift and dark invasion;
The women say that not one stranger told
A reason for his coming. The intrusion
Was not for devastation:
Peace is apparent still on hearth and field.


Yet all the city is a haunted place.
Man meeting man speaks cautiously. Old friends
Close up the candid looks upon their face.
There is no warmth in hands accepting hands;
Each ponders, 'Better hide myself in case
Those strangers have set up their homes in minds
I used to walk in. Better draw the blinds
Even if the strangers haunt in my own house.'

# D. H. LAWRENCE

## *Letter from Town: the Almond Tree*

*Tender for a change.*

You promised to send me some violets. Did you forget?
  White ones and blue ones from under the orchard hedge?
  Sweet dark purple, and white ones mixed for a pledge
Of our early love that hardly has opened yet.


Here there's an almond-tree—you have never seen
  Such a one in the north—it flowers on the street, and I
    stand
  Every day by the fence to look up at the flowers that
    expand
At rest in the blue, and wonder at what they mean.


Under the almond-tree, the happy lands
  Provence, Japan, and Italy repose;
  And passing feet are chatter and clapping of those
Who play around us, country girls clapping their hands.


You, my love, the foremost in a flowered gown,
  All your unbearable tenderness, you with the laughter
  Startled upon your eyes now so wide with hereafter,
You with loose hands of abandonment hanging down.

59

# Discord in Childhood

Outside the house an ash-tree hung its terrible whips,
And at night when the wind rose, the lash of the tree
Shrieked and slashed the wind, as a ship's
Weird rigging in a storm shrieks hideously.

Within the house two voices arose, a slender lash
Whistling she-delirious rage, and the dreadful sound
Of a male thong booming and bruising, until it had drowned
The other voice in a silence of blood, 'neath the noise of the ash.

# Baby Running Barefoot

When the white feet of the baby beat across the grass
The little white feet nod like white flowers in a wind,
They poise and run like puffs of wind that pass
Over water where the weeds are thinned.

And the sight of their white playing in the grass
Is winsome as a robin's song, so fluttering;
Or like two butterflies that settle on a glass
Cup for a moment, soft little wing-beats uttering.

And I wish that the baby would tack across here to me
Like a wind-shadow running on a pond, so she could stand
With two little bare white feet upon my knee
And I could feel her feet in either hand

Cool as syringa buds in morning hours,
Or firm and silken as young peony flowers.

# Snake

A snake came to my water-trough
On a hot, hot day, and I in pyjamas for the heat,
To drink there.

In the deep, strange-scented shade of the great dark carob-tree
I came down the steps with my pitcher
And must wait, must stand and wait, for there he was at the
    trough before me.

He reached down from a fissure in the earth-wall in the
    gloom
And trailed his yellow-brown slackness soft-bellied down, over
    the edge of the stone trough
And rested his throat upon the stone bottom,
And where the water had dripped from the tap, in a small
    clearness,
He sipped with his straight mouth,
Softly drank through his straight gums, into his slack long
    body,
Silently.

Someone was before me at my water-trough,
And I, like a second comer, waiting.
He lifted his head from his drinking, as cattle do,
And looked at me vaguely, as drinking cattle do,
And flickered his two-forked tongue from his lips, and mused a
    moment,
And stooped and drank a little more,
Being earth-brown, earth-golden from the burning bowels of
    the earth
On the day of Sicilian July, with Etna smoking.

The voice of my education said to me
He must be killed,
For in Sicily the black, black snakes are innocent, the gold are
  venomous.


And voices in me said, If you were a man
You would take a stick and break him now, and finish him
  off.


But must I confess how I liked him,
How glad I was he had come like a guest in quiet, to drink at
  my water-trough
And depart peaceful, pacified, and thankless,
Into the burning bowels of this earth?


Was it cowardice, that I dared not kill him?
Was it perversity, that I longed to talk to him?
Was it humility, to feel so honoured?
I felt so honoured.


And yet those voices:
*If you were not afraid, you would kill him!*
And truly I was afraid, I was most afraid,
But even so, honoured still more
That he should seek my hospitality
From out the dark door of the secret earth.


He drank enough
And lifted his head, dreamily, as one who has drunken,
And flickered his tongue like a forked night on the air, so
  black,
Seeming to lick his lips,
And looked around like a god, unseeing, into the air,

And slowly turned his head,
And slowly, very slowly, as if thrice adream,
Proceeded to draw his slow length curving round
And climb again the broken bank of my wall-face.
And as he put his head into that dreadful hole,
And as he slowly drew up, snake-easing his shoulders, and
    entered farther,
A sort of horror, a sort of protest against his withdrawing into
    that horrid black hole,
Deliberately going into the blackness, and slowly drawing
    himself after,
Overcame me now his back was turned.


I looked round, I put down my pitcher,
I picked up a clumsy log
And threw it at the water-trough with a clatter.


I think it did not hit him,
But suddenly that part of him that was left behind convulsed in
    undignified haste,
Writhed like lightning, and was gone
Into the black hole, the earth-lipped fissure in the wall-
    front,
At which, in the intense still noon, I stared with fascination.


And immediately I regretted it.
I thought how paltry, how vulgar, what a mean act!
I despised myself and the voices of my accursed human
    education.


And I thought of the albatross,
And I wished he would come back, my snake.

For he seemed to me again like a king,
Like a king in exile, uncrowned in the underworld,
Now due to be crowned again.

And so, I missed my chance with one of the lords
Of life.
And I have something to expiate;
A pettiness.


## Humming-bird

I can imagine, in some other world
Primeval-dumb, far back
In that most awful stillness, that only gasped and hummed,
Humming-birds raced down the avenues.

Before anything had a soul,
While life was a heave of matter, half inanimate,
This little bit chipped off in brilliance
And went whizzing through the slow, vast, succulent stems.

I believe there were no flowers then,
In the world where the humming-bird flashes ahead of
    creation.
I believe he pierced the slow vegetable veins with his long
    beak.

Probably he was big
As mosses, and little lizards, they say, were once big.
Probably he was a jabbing, terrifying monster.

We look at him through the wrong end of the long telescope of
    Time,
Luckily for us.

## Let Us Be Men

For God's sake, let us be men
not monkeys minding machines
or sitting with our tails curled
while the machine amuses us, the radio or film or gramo-
    phone.

Monkeys with a bland grin on our faces.——

## The Optimist

    The optimist builds himself safe inside a cell
    and paints the inside walls sky-blue
    and blocks up the door
    and says he's in heaven.

## ALUN LEWIS

## In Hospital : Poona

    Last night I did not fight for sleep
    But lay awake from midnight while the world
    Turned its slow features to the moving deep
    Of darkness, till I knew that you were furled,

    Beloved, in the same dark watch as I.
    And sixty degrees of longitude beside
    Vanished as though a swan in ecstasy
    Had spanned the distance from your sleeping side.

And like to swan or moon the whole of Wales
Glided within the parish of my care:
I saw the green tide leap on Cardigan
Your red yacht riding like a legend there,

And the great mountains, Dafydd and Llewelyn,
Plynlimmon, Cader Idris and Eryri
Threshing the darkness back from head and fin,
And also the small nameless mining valley

Whose slopes are scratched with streets and sprawling
    graves
Dark in the lap of firwoods and great boulders
Where you lay waiting, listening to the waves—
My hot hands touched your white despondent shoulders

—And then ten thousand miles of daylight grew
Between us, and I heard the wild daws crake
In India's starving throat; whereat I knew
That Time upon the heart can break
But love survives the venom of the snake.

# C. DAY LEWIS

## *Nearing Again the Legendary Isle*

Nearing again the legendary isle
Where sirens sang and mariners were skinned,
We wonder now what was there to beguile
That such stout fellows left their bones behind.

Those chorus-girls are surely past their prime,
Voices grow shrill and paint is wearing thin,
Lips that sealed up the sense from gnawing time
Now beg the favour with a graveyard grin.

We have no flesh to spare and they can't bite,
Hunger and sweat have stripped us to the bone;
A skeleton crew we toil upon the tide
And mock the theme-song meant to lure us on:

No need to stop the ears, avert the eyes
From purple rhetoric of evening skies.


## LOUIS MACNEICE

### Brother Fire

When our brother Fire was having his dog's day
Jumping the London streets with millions of tin cans
Clanking at his tail, we heard some shadow say
'Give the dog a bone'—and so we gave him ours;
Night after night we watched him slaver and crunch
    away
The beams of human life, the tops of topless towers.

Which gluttony of his for us was Lenten fare
Who mother-naked, suckled with sparks, were chill

Though cotted in a grill of sizzling air
Striped like a convict—black, yellow and red;
Thus we were weaned to knowledge of the Will
That wills the natural world but wills us dead.


O delicate walker, babbler, dialectician Fire,
O enemy and image of ourselves,
Did we not on those mornings after the All Clear,
When you were looting shops in elemental joy
And singing as you swarmed up city block and spire,
Echo your thoughts in ours? 'Destroy! Destroy!'


## Entirely

If we could get the hang of it entirely
    It would take too long;
All we know is the splash of words in passing
    And falling twigs of song,
And when we try to eavesdrop on the great
    Presences it is rarely
That by a stroke of luck we can appropriate
    Even a phrase entirely.


If we could find our happiness entirely
    In somebody else's arms
We should not fear the spears of the spring nor the cities'
    Yammering fire alarms
But, as it is, the spears each year go through
    Our flesh and almost hourly
Bell or siren banishes the blue
    Eyes of Love entirely.

And if the world were black or white entirely
    And all the charts were plain
Instead of a mad weir of tigerish waters,
    A prism of delight and pain,
We might be surer where we wished to go
    Or again we might be merely
Bored but in brute reality there is no
    Road that is right entirely.

*March, 1940*

# CHARLES MADGE

## *Fortune*

The natural silence of a tree
The motion of a mast upon the fresh-tossing sea
Now foam-inclined, now to the sun with dignity

Or the stone brow of a mountain
Regarded from a town, or the curvet fountain
Or one street-stopped in wonder at the fountain

Or a great cloud entering the room of the sky
Napoleon of his century
Heard come to knowing music consciously

Such, not us, reflect and have their day
We are but vapour of today
Unless love's chance fall on us and call us away

As the wind takes what it can
And blowing on the fortunate face, reveals the man.

# EDWIN MUIR

## *Merlin*

O Merlin in your crystal cave
Deep in the diamond of the day,
Will there ever be a singer
Whose music will smooth away
The furrow drawn by Adam's finger
Across the meadow and the wave?
Or a runner who'll outrun
Man's long shadow driving on,
Break through the gate of memory
And hang the apple on the tree?
Will your magic ever show
The sleeping bride shut in her bower,
The day wreathed in its mound of snow
And Time locked in his tower?

## *The Return*

The doors flapped open in Ulysses' house,
The lolling latches gave to every hand,
Let traitor, babbler, tout and bargainer in.
The rooms and passages resounded
With ease and chaos of a public market,
The walls mere walls to lean on as you talked,
Spat on the floor, surveyed some newcomer
With an absent eye. There you could be yourself.

Dust in the nooks, weeds nodding in the yard,
The thick walls crumbling. Even the cattle came
About the doors with mild familiar stare
As if this were their place.
All round the island stretched the clean blue sea.


Sole at the house's heart Penelope
Sat at her chosen task, endless undoing
Of endless doing, endless weaving, unweaving,
In the clean chamber. Still her loom ran empty
Day after day. She thought: 'Here I do nothing
Or less than nothing, making an emptiness
Amid disorder, weaving, unweaving the lie
The day demands. Ulysses, this is duty,
To do and undo, to keep a vacant gate
Where order and right and hope and peace can enter.
Oh will you ever return? Or are you dead,
And this wrought emptiness my ultimate emptiness?'

.

She wove and unwove and wove and did not know
That even then Ulysses on the long
And winding road of the world was on his way.


# The Animals

They do not live in the world,
Are not in time and space.
From birth to death hurled
No word do they have, not one
To plant a foot upon,
Were never in any place.

For with name the world was called
Out of the empty air,
With names was built and walled,
Line and circle and square,
Dust and emerald;
Snatched from deceiving death
By the articulate breath.

But these have never trod
Twice the familiar track,
Never never turned back
Into the memoried day.
All is new and near
In the unchanging Here
Of the fifth great day of God,
That shall remain the same,
Never shall pass away.

On the sixth day we came.

## WILFRED OWEN

## *Dulce et Decorum Est*

Bent double, like old beggars under sacks,
Knock-kneed, coughing like hags, we cursed through sludge,
Till on the haunting flares we turned our backs,
And towards our distant rest began to trudge.
Men marched asleep. Many had lost their boots,
But limped on, blood-shod. All went lame, all blind;
Drunk with fatigue; deaf even to the hoots
Of gas-shells dropping softly behind.

Gas! GAS! Quick, boys!—An ecstasy of fumbling,
Fitting the clumsy helmets just in time,
But someone still was yelling out and stumbling
And floundering like a man in fire or lime.—
Dim through the misty panes and thick green light,
As under a green sea, I saw him drowning.

In all my dreams before my helpless sight
He plunges at me, guttering, choking, drowning.

If in some smothering dreams, you too could pace
Behind the wagon that we flung him in,
And watch the white eyes writhing in his face,
His hanging face, like a devil's sick of sin;
If you could hear, at every jolt, the blood
Come gargling from the froth-corrupted lungs,
Bitter as the cud
Of vile, incurable sores on innocent tongues,—
My friend, you would not tell with such high zest
To children ardent for some desperate glory,
The old Lie: Dulce et decorum est
Pro patria mori.

## Futility

Move him into the sun—
    Gently its touch awoke him once,
    At home, whispering of fields unsown.
    Always it woke him, even in France,
    Until this morning and this snow.
    If anything might rouse him now
    The kind old sun will know.

73

Think how it wakes the seeds,—
Woke, once, the clays of a cold star.
Are limbs, so dear-achieved, are sides,
Full-nerved—still warm—too hard to stir?
Was it for this the clay grew tall?
—O what made fatuous sunbeams toil
To break earth's sleep at all?

## Anthem for Doomed Youth

What passing-bells for these who die as cattle?
   Only the monstrous anger of the guns.
   Only the stuttering rifles' rapid rattle
Can patter out their hasty orisons.
No mockeries for them from prayers or bells,
   Nor any voice of mourning save the choirs,—
The shrill, demented choirs of wailing shells;
   And bugles calling for them from sad shires.

What candles may be held to speed them all?
   Not in the hands of boys, but in their eyes
Shall shine the holy glimmers of good-byes.
   The pallor of girls' brows shall be their pall;
Their flowers the tenderness of silent minds,
And each slow dusk a drawing-down of blinds.

## EZRA POUND

## A Pact

I make a pact with you, Walt Whitman—
I have detested you long enough.

I come to you as a grown child
Who has had a pig-headed father;
I am old enough now to make friends.
It was you that broke the new wood,
Now is a time for carving.
We have one sap and one root—
Let there be commerce between us.


## Salutation

O generation of the thoroughly smug and thoroughly un-
    comfortable,
I have seen fishermen picnicking in the sun,
I have seen them with untidy families,
I have seen their smiles full of teeth and heard ungainly laughter.
And I am happier than you are,
And they were happier than I am;
And the fish swim in the lake and do not even own clothing.


## A Girl

The tree has entered my hands,
The sap has ascended my arms,
The tree has grown in my breast—
Downward,
The branches grow out of me, like arms.

Tree you are,
Moss you are,
You are violets with wind above them.
A child—*so* high—you are,
And all this is folly to the world.

# F. T. PRINCE

## *To a Man on his Horse*

Only the Arab stallion will I
Envy you. Along the water
You dance him with the morning on his flanks.
In the frosty morning that his motions flatter
He kindles and where the winter's in the wood
I watch you dance him out on delicate shanks.
And lashes fall on a dark eye,
He sheds a silvery mane, he shapes
His thin nostrils like a fop's.
And to do honour to his whiteness
In remembrance of his ancient blood
I have wished to become his groom
And so his smouldering body comb
In a simple and indecorous sweetness.


# KATHLEEN RAINE

## *The Moment*

To write down all I contain at this moment
I would pour the desert through an hour-glass,
The sea through a water-clock,
Grain by grain and drop by drop
Let in the trackless, measureless, mutable seas and sands.

For earth's days and nights are breaking over me
The tides and sands are running through me,
And I have only two hands and a heart to hold the desert and
    the sea.

What can I contain of it? It escapes and eludes me
The tides wash me away
The desert shifts under my feet.

## JOHN CROWE RANSOM

### *Old Man Playing with Children*

A discreet householder exclaims on the grandsire
In warpaint and feathers, with fierce grandsons and axes
Dancing round a backyard fire of boxes:
'Watch grandfather, he'll set the house on fire.'

But I will unriddle for you the thought of his mind,
An old one you cannot open with conversation.
What animates the thin legs in risky motion?
Mixes the snow on the head with snow on the wind?

'Grandson, grandsire. We are equally boy and boy.
Do not offer your reclining-chair and slippers
With tedious old women talking in wrappers.
This life is not good but in danger and in joy.

'It is you the elder to these and younger to me
Who are penned as slaves by properties and causes
And never walk from your shaped insupportable houses
And shamefully, when boys shout, go in and flee.

'May God forgive me, I know your middling ways,
Having taken care and performed ignominies unreckoned
Between the first brief childhood and the brief second,
But I will be the more honourable in these days.'


## Winter Remembered

Two evils, monstrous either one apart,
Possessed me, and were long and loath at going:
A cry of Absence, Absence, in the heart,
And in the wood the furious winter blowing.

Think not, when fire was bright upon my bricks,
And past the tight boards hardly a wind could enter,
I glowed like them, the simple burning sticks,
Far from my cause, my proper heat and centre.

Better to walk forth in the murderous air
And wash my wound in the snows; that would be healing;
Because my heart would throb less painful there,
Being caked with cold, and past the smart of feeling.

And where I went, the hugest winter blast
Would have this body bowed, these eyeballs streaming,
And though I think this heart's blood froze not fast
It ran too small to spare one drop for dreaming.

Dear love, these fingers that had known your touch,
And tied our separate forces first together,
Were ten poor idiot fingers not worth much,
Ten frozen parsnips hanging in the weather.

## Piazza Piece

—I am a gentleman in a dustcoat trying
To make you hear. Your ears are soft and small
And listen to an old man not at all,
They want the young men's whispering and sighing.
But see the roses on your trellis dying
And hear the spectral singing of the moon;
For I must have my lovely lady soon,
I am a gentleman in a dustcoat trying.

—I am a lady young in beauty waiting
Until my truelove comes, and then we kiss.
But what grey man among the vines is this
Whose words are dry and faint as in a dream?
Back from my trellis, Sir, before I scream!
I am a lady young in beauty waiting.


## Blue Girls

Twirling your blue skirts, travelling the sward
Under the towers of your seminary,
Go listen to your teachers old and contrary
Without believing a word.

Tie the white fillets then about your hair
And think no more of what will come to pass
Than bluebirds that go walking on the grass
And chattering on the air.

Practise your beauty, blue girls, before it fail;
And I will cry with my loud lips and publish
Beauty which all our power shall never establish,
It is so frail.

For I could tell you a story which is true;
I know a lady with a terrible tongue,
Blear eyes fallen from blue,
All her perfections tarnished—yet it is not long
Since she was lovelier than any of you.

## Dead Boy

The little cousin is dead, by foul subtraction,
A green bough from Virginia's aged tree,
And none of the county kin like the transaction
Nor some of the world of outer dark, like me.

A boy not beautiful, nor good, nor clever,
A black cloud full of storms too hot for keeping,
A sword beneath his mother's heart—yet never
Woman bewept her babe as this is weeping.

A pig with a pasty face, so I had said.
Squealing for cookies, kinned by pure pretence
With a noble house. But the little man quite dead,
I can see the forbears' antique lineaments.

The elder men have strode by the box of death
To the wide flag porch, and muttering low send round
The bruit of the day. O friendly waste of breath!
Their hearts are hurt with a deep dynastic wound.

He was pale and little, the foolish neighbours say;
The first-fruits, saith the Preacher, the Lord hath taken;
But this was the old tree's late branch wrenched away,
Grieving the sapless limbs, the shorn and shaken.

# LYNETTE ROBERTS

## *The Seasons*

Spring which has its appeal in ghosts,
Youth, resurrection, cleansing of the soil,
And in dormant roots already considered,
Stirs, with the sharpening of branches
Challenges heart to do that which it cannot,
Sustain overwork, overthought, overlove.
It clears a path for hope: reinstates
Faith, which we had too easily omitted
With death, in the caustic months of the year.


Summer proclaims joy, laughter before its
Arrival: and deceives us into malice
With its non appearance. It suggests
A romance that we have not received,
Sunny balconies in the mind: the seldom
Forgotten perfect island summer with its
Warm haze on flesh, flower, and hide:
The blossoming of their structure, fragrance
And appeal, from their own root recorded.


Autumn comes strutting in like a cockerel,
Red, blue, yellow and brown. It disintegrates
Our purpose of singular thought; destroys
Relationships: and cuts the sap of pride
Ruthlessly. Those who survive retain one heart

And voice. Yet autumn with contrawise motion
Shields the creative mind with covering of leaves,
Settles and matures dormant growth which will
Reappear, under the hard skies of spring.

Winter exceeds the year with impunity:
Devours us of all greed: and freezes
That residue. It upholds that which is not:
Which is, the blaze of summer biting
Into our nature for a future reappeal.
Winter intones loss of all things:
Is the next step to death which is loneliness:
Comfort and warmth to be found around our own
Heart and grate, within the steel ribs of this age.

# SIEGFRIED SASSOON

## *Devotion to Duty*

I was near the King that day. I saw him snatch
And briskly scan the G.H.Q. dispatch.
Thick-voiced, he read it out. (His face was grave.)
'This officer advanced with the first wave,

'And when our first objective had been gained,
'(Though wounded twice), reorganized the line:
'The spirit of the troops was by his fine
'Example most effectively sustained.'

He gripped his beard; then closed his eyes and said,
'Bathsheba must be warned that he is dead.
'Send for her. I will be the first to tell
'This wife how her heroic husband fell.'

82

# Brevities

I am that man who with a luminous look
Sits up at night to write a ruminant book.

I am that man who with a furrowing frown
Thinks harshly of the world—and corks it down.

I am that man who loves to ride alone
When landscapes wear his mind's autumnal tone.

I am that man who, having lived his day,
Looks once on life and goes his wordless way.


# Eulogy of my House

House, though you've harboured grave-yards full of lives
Since on your first foundations walls were built,
In your essential atmosphere survives
No sense of men's malignity and guilt.
Bad times you must have known, and human wrongness;
Yet your plain wisdom leaves it all behind you,
Within whose walls tranquillity and strongness
Keep watch on life. Dependable I find you.

Much good has been your making. I can feel
That when your ghosts revisit you they steal
From room to room like moonlight long ago:
And if some voice from silence haunts my head
I only wonder who it was that said—
'House, I am here because I loved you so.'

## Gloria Mundi

Who needs words in autumn woods
When colour concludes decay?
There old stories are told in glories
For winds to scatter away.

Wisdom narrows where downland barrows
Image the world's endeavour.
There time's tales are as light that fails
On faces fading for ever.


## MARTIN SEYMOUR-SMITH

## Green Wall my Grave

This green wall to which I turn for sleep
  Has told my curse upon its shining face.
In it, true-reflected, I have seen
  The land that is my dwelling-place.

'O grave, O grave, when will you let me sleep?'
  All night I asked; the wall became the sea—
My drowned past selves came up, each one alone,
  And with the quarter-striking bells, mocked me.

The firelight flickered on the wall,
  Showed me the houses I had known and lost:
But I was dead, and as I watched
  The bugle sounded my last post.

But in this death at last I knew
   The living of a perfect grief and once again
I held my weeping love, and from her tears
   I now return, in this thin rain

To my green wall. The fire is out,
   The bells are cold as still they sound
The quarters to a light I wait not for
   In a dark which I have not found.

Then comes the dawn: the early trumpet
   Blows the dead fire ashes far away,
And as I sleepless grieving rise
   I realise that to-day

We storm our enemies the flowers:
   I strike them down to make my woman weep,
And with her crying still I cry
   'O grave, O grave, when will you let me sleep?'

# EDITH SITWELL (more interested in experiment - thus difficult)

## *How Many Heavens . . .*

The emeralds are singing on the grasses
And in the trees the bells of the long cold are ringing,—
My blood seems changed to emeralds like the spears
Of grass beneath the earth piercing and singing.

The flame of the first blade
Is an angel piercing through the earth to sing
'God is everything!
The grass within the grass, the angel in the angel, flame
Within the flame, and He is the green shade that came
To be the heart of shade.'

The grey-beard angel of the stone,
Who has grown wise with age, cried 'Not alone
Am I within my silence,—God is the stone in the still stone, the
        silence laid
In the heart of silence' . . . then, above the glade

The yellow straws of light
Whereof the sun has built his nest, cry 'Bright
Is the world, the yellow straw
My brother,—God is the straw within the straw:—All things
        are Light.'

He is the sea of ripeness and the sweet apple's emerald lore.
So you, my flame of grass, my root of the world from which
        all Spring shall grow,
O you, my hawthorn bough of the stars, now leaning low
Through the day, for your flowers to kiss my lips, shall know
He is the core of the heart of love, and He, beyond labouring
        seas, our ultimate shore.


## Girl and Butterfly

I, an old man,
Bent like Ixion on my broken wheel the world,
Stare at the dust and scan
What has been made of it . . . and my companion

Shadow, born with a wolfish pelt—
Grey dress to wear against the invincible cold
Sits at my feet. . . . We scan the old
And young, we stare at the old woman
Who bears a stone in her breast
That will not let her rest
Because it once was a world in the grey dawn
When sap and blood were one.


We stare at the young girl chasing a yellow butterfly
On the summer roads that lead from Nothing to Nowhere.


What golden racers, young winds, have gone! For the dust like
      a great wave
Breaks over them—the shade of mortality lying
On the golden hand (the calyx outshining all flowers)—
The hand that drew the chart of the undiscovered,
And the smile for which great golden heroes marched with the
      pride
And pomp of waves—and like the waves they died.
The words that drew from the shade
A planetary system:
                        These are gone—


And the Grey Man that waits on the Road from Nothing to
      Nowhere
Does not care how the breezes and butterflies move their four
      wings—
And now the old woman who once was a world and my earth,
Lies like time upon my heart, or a drift of the grey dust.


But the young girl chases the yellow butterfly
Happiness . . . what is the dust that lies on its wings?

Is it from far away
From the distance that lies between lover and lover, their minds
    never meeting—
Like the bright continents?—are Asia, Africa, and Cathay
But golden flowers that shine in the fields of summer—
As quickly dying?


## STEPHEN SPENDER

### *My Parents Kept me from Children who were Rough*

My parents kept me from children who were rough
And who threw words like stones and who wore torn clothes.
Their thighs showed through rags. They ran in the street
And climbed cliffs and stripped by the country streams.


I feared more than tigers their muscles like iron
And their jerking hands and their knees tight on my arms.
I feared the salt coarse pointing of those boys
Who copied my lisp behind me on the road.


They were lithe, they sprang out behind hedges
Like dogs to bark at our world. They threw mud
And I looked another way, pretending to smile.
I longed to forgive them, yet they never smiled.

# Shapes of Death Haunt Life

Shapes of death haunt life,
Neurosis eclipsing each in special shadow:
Unrequited love not solving
The need to become another's body
Wears black invisibility:
The greed for property
Heaps a skyscraper over the breathing ribs:
The speedlines of dictators
Cut their own stalks:
From afar, we watch the best of us—
Whose adored desire was to die for the world.


Ambition is my death. That flat thin flame
I feed, that plants my shadow. This prevents love
And offers love of being loved or loving.
The humorous self-forgetful drunkenness
It hates, demands the pyramids
Be built. Who can prevent
His death's industry, which when he sleeps
Throws up its towers? And conceals in slackness
The dreams of revolution, the birth of death?


Also the swallows by autumnal instinct
Comfort us with their effortless exhaustion
In great unguided flight to their complete South.
There on my fancied pyramids they lodge
But for delight, their whole compulsion.
Not teaching me to love, but soothing my eyes:
Not saving me from death, but saving me from speech.

# DYLAN THOMAS

## *The Hunchback in the Park*

The hunchback in the park
A solitary mister
Propped between trees and water
From the opening of the garden lock
That lets the trees and water enter
Until the Sunday sombre bell at dark

Eating bread from a newspaper
Drinking water from the chained cup
That the children filled with gravel
In the fountain basin where I sailed my ship
Slept at night in a dog kennel
But nobody chained him up.

Like the park birds he came early
Like the water he sat down
And Mister they called Hey mister
The truant boys from the town
Running when he had heard them clearly
On out of sound

Past lake and rockery
Laughing when he shook his paper
Hunchbacked in mockery
Through the loud zoo of the willow groves
Dodging the park keeper
With his stick that picked up leaves.

And the old dog sleeper
Alone between nurses and swans
While the boys among willows
Made the tigers jump out of their eyes
To roar on the rockery stones
And the groves were blue with sailors

Made all day until bell time
A woman figure without fault
Straight as a young elm
Straight and tall from his crooked bones
That she might stand in the night
After the locks and chains

All night in the unmade park
After the railings and shrubberies
The birds the grass the trees the lake
And the wild boys innocent as strawberries
Had followed the hunchback
To his kennel in the dark.

## Fern Hill

*Delight in words.*
*Visionary.*

Now as I was young and easy under the apple boughs
About the lilting house and happy as the grass was green,
    The night above the dingle starry,
      Time let me hail and climb
    Golden in the heydays of his eyes,
And honoured among wagons I was prince of the apple towns
And once below a time I lordly had the trees and leaves
      Trail with daisies and barley
    Down the rivers of the windfall light.

And as I was green and carefree, famous among the barns
About the happy yard and singing as the farm was home,
In the sun that is young once only,
Time let me play and be
Golden in the mercy of his means,
And green and golden I was huntsman and herdsman, the calves
Sang to my horn, the foxes on the hills barked clear and cold,
And the sabbath rang slowly
In the pebbles of the holy streams.

*inverted* All the sun long it was running, it was lovely, the hay
Fields high as the house, the tunes from the chimneys, was air
And playing, lovely and watery
And fire green as grass.
And nightly under the simple stars
As I rode to sleep the owls were bearing the farm away,
*inverted* All the moon long I heard, blessed among stables, the nightjars
Flying with the ricks, and the horses
Flashing into the dark.

And then to awake, and the farm, like a wanderer white
With the dew, come back, the cock on his shoulder: it was all
Shining, it was Adam and maiden,
The sky gathered again
And the sun grew round that very day.
So it must have been after the birth of the simple light
In the first, spinning place, the spellbound horses walking warm
Out of the whinnying green stable
On to the fields of praise.

And honoured among foxes and pheasants by the gay house
Under the new made clouds and happy as the heart was long,
In the sun born over and over,
I ran my heedless ways,
My wishes raced through the house high hay

*compound adj.*

And nothing I cared, at my sky blue trades, that time allows
In all his tuneful turning so few and such morning songs
    Before the children green and golden
        Follow him out of grace,

Nothing I cared, in the lamb white days, that time would take me
Up to the swallow thronged loft by the shadow of my hand,
    In the moon that is always rising,
        Nor that riding to sleep
    I should hear him fly with the high fields
And wake to the farm for ever fled from the childless land.
Oh as I was young and easy in the mercy of his means,
        Time held me green and dying
    Though I sang in my chains like the sea.

# EDWARD THOMAS

## *Tears*

It seems I have no tears left. They should have fallen—
Their ghosts, if tears have ghosts, did fall—that day
When twenty hounds streamed by me, not yet combed out
But still all equals in their rage of gladness
Upon the scent, made one, like a great dragon
In Blooming Meadow that bends towards the sun
And once bore hops: and on that other day
When I stepped out from the double-shadowed Tower
Into an April morning, stirring and sweet
And warm. Strange solitude was there and silence.
A mightier charm than any in the Tower
Possessed the courtyard. They were changing guard,

Soldiers in line, young English countrymen,
Fair-haired and ruddy, in white tunics. Drums
And fifes were playing 'The British Grenadiers'.
Then men, the music piercing that solitude
And silence, told me truths I had not dreamed,
And have forgotten since their beauty passed.

## *February Afternoon*

Men heard this roar of parleying starlings, saw,
   A thousand years ago even as now,
   Black rooks with white gulls following the plough
So that the first are last until a caw
Commands that last are first again,—a law
   Which was of old when one, like me, dreamed how
   A thousand years might dust lie on his brow
Yet thus would birds do between hedge and shaw.

Time swims before me, making as a day
   A thousand years, while the broad ploughland oak
   Roars mill-like and men strike and bear the stroke
Of war as ever, audacious or resigned,
And God still sits aloft in the array
   That we have wrought him, stone-deaf and stone-blind.

# ARTHUR WALEY

## *Business Men*

Business men boast of their skill and cunning
But in philosophy they are like little children.
Bragging to each other of successful depredations
They neglect to consider the ultimate fate of the body.

What should they know of the Master of Dark Truth
Who saw the wide world in a jade cup,
By illumined conception got clear of Heaven and Earth:
On the chariot of Mutation entered the Gate of Immutability?

Ch'ēn Tzŭ-ang

## Protest in the Sixth Year of Ch'ien Fu
### (A.D. 879)

The hills and rivers of the lowland country
    You have made your battle-ground.
How do you suppose the people who live there
    Will procure 'firewood and hay'?
Do not let me hear you talking together
    About titles and promotions;
For a single general's reputation
    Is made out of ten thousand corpses.

Ts'ao Sung

## Illness

Sad, sad—lean with long illness;
Monotonous, monotonous—days and nights pass.
The summer trees have clad themselves in shade;
The autumn 'lan' already houses the dew.
The eggs that lay in the nest when I took to bed
Have changed into little birds and flown away.
The worm that then lay hidden in its hole
Has hatched into a cricket sitting on the tree.
The Four Seasons go on for ever and ever:
In all Nature nothing stops to rest
Even for a moment. Only the sick man's heart
Deep down still aches as of old!

Po Chü-i

# The Harper of Chao

The singers have hushed their notes of clear song:
The red sleeves of the dancers are motionless.
Hugging his lute, the old harper of Chao
Rocks and sways as he touches the five chords.
The loud notes swell and scatter abroad:
'Sa, sa,' like wind blowing the rain.
The soft notes dying almost to nothing:
'Ch'ieh, ch'ieh,' like the voice of ghosts talking.
Now as glad as the magpie's lucky song:
Again bitter as the gibbon's ominous cry.
His ten fingers have no fixed note:
Up and down—'kung', chih, and yü.[1]
And those who sit and listen to the tune he plays
Of soul and body lose the mastery.
And those who pass that way as he plays the tune,
Suddenly stop and cannot raise their feet.

Alas, alas that the ears of common men
Should love the modern and not love the old.
Thus it is that the harp in the green window
Day by day is covered deeper with dust.

*Po Chü-i*

[1] Tonic, dominant and superdominant of the ancient five-note scale.

# Madly singing in the Mountains

There is no one among men that has not a special failing :
And my failing consists in writing verses.
I have broken away from the thousand ties of life:
But this infirmity still remains behind.
Each time that I look at a fine landscape,
Each time that I meet a loved friend,
I raise my voice and recite a stanza of poetry
And am glad as though a God had crossed my path.
Ever since the day I was banished to Hsün-yang
Half my time I have lived among the hills.
And often, when I have finished a new poem,
Alone I climb the road to the Eastern Rock.
I lean my body on the banks of white stone:
I pull down with my hands a green cassia branch.
My mad singing startles the valleys and hills:
The apes and birds all come to peep.
Fearing to become a laughing-stock to the world,
I choose a place that is unfrequented by men.

Po Chü-i

# The Red Cockatoo

Sent as a present from Annam—
A red cockatoo.
Coloured like the peach-tree blossom,
Speaking with the speech of men.
And they did to it what is always done
To the learned and eloquent.
They took a cage with stout bars
And shut it up inside.

Po Chü-i

# W. B. YEATS

## *September 1913*

What need you, being come to sense,
But fumble in a greasy till
And add the halfpence to the pence
And prayer to shivering prayer, until
You have dried the marrow from the bone;
For men were born to pray and save:
Romantic Ireland's dead and gone,
It's with O'Leary in the grave.

Yet they were of a different kind
The names that chilled your childish play,
They have gone about the world like wind,
But little time had they to pray
For whom the hangman's rope was spun,
And what, God help us, could they save:
Romantic Ireland's dead and gone,
It's with O'Leary in the grave.

Was it for this the wild geese spread
The grey wing upon every tide;
For this that all the blood was shed,
For this Edward Fitzgerald died,
And Robert Emmet and Wolfe Tone,
All that delirium of the brave;
Romantic Ireland's dead and gone,
It's with O'Leary in the grave.

Yet could we turn the years again,
And call those exiles as they were,
In all their loneliness and pain
You'd cry, 'Some woman's yellow hair
Has maddened every mother's son:
They weighed so lightly what they gave,
But let them be, they're dead and gone,
They're with O'Leary in the grave.'

## Sailing to Byzantium

### I

That is no country for old men. The young
In one another's arms, birds in the trees,
—Those dying generations—at their song,
The salmon-falls, the mackerel-crowded seas,
Fish, flesh, or fowl, commend all summer long
Whatever is begotten, born, and dies.
Caught in that sensual music all neglect
Monuments of unaging intellect.

*Best verse
in poem.*

### II

*If that were all —*

An aged man is but a paltry thing,
A tattered coat upon a stick, unless
Soul clap its hands and sing, and louder sing
For every tatter in its mortal dress,
Nor is there singing school but studying
Monuments of its own magnificence;
And therefore I have sailed the seas and come
To the holy city of Byzantium.

## III

O sages standing in God's holy fire
As in the gold mosaic of a wall,
Come from the holy fire, perne in a gyre,
And be the singing masters of my soul.
Consume my heart away; sick with desire
And fastened to a dying animal
It knows not what it is; and gather me
Into the artifice of eternity.

## IV

Once out of nature I shall never take *Reincarnation*
My bodily form from any natural thing,
But such a form as Grecian goldsmiths make
Of hammered gold and gold enamelling
To keep a drowsy emperor awake;
Or set upon a golden bough to sing
To lords and ladies of Byzantium
Of what is past, or passing, or to come.

## Stream and Sun at Glendalough

Through intricate motions ran
Stream and gliding sun
And all my heart seemed gay:
Some stupid thing that I had done
Made my attention stray.

Repentance keeps my heart impure;
But what am I that dare
Fancy that I can
Better conduct myself or have more
Sense than a common man?

What motion of the sun or stream
Or eyelid shot the gleam
That pierced my body through?
What made me live like these that seem
Self-born, born anew?


# ANDREW YOUNG

## *A Prehistoric Camp*

It was the time of year
  Pale lambs leap with thick leggings on
Over small hills that are not there,
  That I climbed Eggardon.

The hedgerows still were bare,
  None ever knew so late a year;
Birds built their nests in the open air, *hedges with no leaves*
  Love conquering their fear.

But there on the hill-crest,
  Where only larks or stars look down,
Earthworks exposed a vaster nest,
  Its race of men long flown.

## Cuckoos

When coltsfoot withers and begins to wear
Long silver locks instead of golden hair,
And fat red catkins from black poplars fall
And on the ground like caterpillars crawl,
And bracken lifts up slender arms and wrists
And stretches them, unfolding sleepy fists,
The cuckoos in a few well-chosen words
Tell they give Easter eggs to the small birds.


## A Windy Day

This wind brings all dead things to life,
Branches that lash the air like whips
And dead leaves rolling in a hurry
Or peering in a rabbit's bury
Or trying to push down a tree;
Gates that fly open to the wind
And close again behind,
And fields that are a flowing sea
And make the cattle look like ships;
Straws glistening and stiff
Lying on air as on a shelf
And pond that leaps to leave itself;
And feathers too that rise and float,
Each feather changed into a bird,
And line-hung sheets that crack and strain;
Even the sun-greened coat,
That through so many winds has served,
The scarecrow struggles to put on again.

# COMMENTARY

W. H. AUDEN (born 1907), one of the most influential poets of his generation, is concerned with the social and psychological diseases of modern civilisation. His language is crisp and self-consciously contemporary, and seems to spring from a natural virtuosity in handling words rather than from intense personal feeling. Notice the impersonality and deliberate anonymity of Auden's world—the famous man in *Who's Who* and the city in *The Capital*.

### 1. WHO'S WHO

A sonnet contrasting the public life of a famous man with his unsatisfied private longings. Notice how the indifference of the loved one (possibly his mother) of the last six lines is expressed in the last three words of the poem.

### 1. CULTURE

The subject of this poem is the social guilt-complex of the ruling class. Nature alone is happy because ignorant; man, through knowledge, has acquired a sense of guilt. In order to protect himself from his knowledge, he has invented culture—literature, team games, music, etc. In this way the leisured classes protect themselves from knowledge of the masses.

*shearwater:* sea-bird with a harsh, scolding cry.

### 2. THE CAPITAL

The city (capital of an unnamed agricultural country) acts as a lure to foreigners and to the farmers' sons. It is a place where people can lose themselves and escape from the compulsions of nature, even though some may be ruined or miserable there.

GEORGE BARKER (born 1913). These are two of the shorter, simpler and more lyrical poems of a writer often obscure and involved.

### 3. MY JOY, MY JOCKEY, MY GABRIEL

A girl's expression of delight in her lover, in which striking and unusual images are drawn together to convey her ecstasy.

## 4. TO MY MOTHER

An expression of love for a bereaved mother in war-time.

*seismic:* like an earthquake. Possibly *Asia* was chosen in line 3 not only because it is the largest of the continents but because the writer associates it with earthquakes.

*Rabelais:* French writer, author of *Gargantua*, associated with laughter and well-being on a grand scale.

JOHN BETJEMAN (born 1906) excels in a kind of light verse in which he describes with mocking nostalgia the life of the suburban well-to-do. His sense of period is unequalled, and the details of style and fashion in the 1920's (the period of *Indoor Games near Newbury*) are authentic.

EDMUND BLUNDEN (born 1896) has published poems of a consistently high quality ever since the 1920's. His work is meditative and scholarly rather than dramatic; its colouring is quiet, not showy. At its best it is the expression of thoughts deeply felt and compressed into well wrought forms. His poetry wears well after successive re-readings, as more superficially brilliant poetry does not.

## 6. THE RECOVERY

Amidst the humble and 'unexalted' life of the fields the writer finds a cure for the 'dark mood' which has possessed him. He realises that the 'high imaginings' induced by contemplating the exalted atmosphere of earlier days are dangerous to his peace of mind.

## 7. ANOTHER ALTAR

A monologue supposed to be spoken by Forgetfulness, an unrecognised minor god. The poem falls into two parts: the first gives a general account of the part played by Forgetfulness in shaping people's lives in unexpected ways; the second gives examples of the good and evil achievements of the God.

*Tanagra:* in Greece, where ancient terra-cotta figurines were discovered.

## 9. IN MY TIME

Some men dwell on the vividly coloured experiences in their past; others, like me, on those of quieter tone. Each is moved by a different kind of memory. All I know is that when the past calls me I must surrender to it. To analyse life is no substitute for living; but rational analysis must be ignored when the moments we dwell on so passionately prove on examination to be of small worth—if, as in my case, the 'silver hour' is nothing more than some war experience which would seem insignificant to others.

10. REPORT ON EXPERIENCE

A controlled and ironic expression of anger at the contrast between life as promised and life as experienced. Although the poem was not published until 1929, it is clear from the second verse that the poet is looking back to the destructive futility of the 1914–1918 war.

NORMAN CAMERON (1905–1953) was a poet whose output was limited (less than sixty short poems, not counting his translations) by scrupulous standards of craftsmanship. He aimed at absolute precision of word and image, and was never satisfied with anything slipshod or inexact. Many of his poems are ironical comments on the curious world in which he found himself and the curious people he found there, himself included. He lived mostly in London, but his work before and during the war took him also to Africa, Europe and the Mediterranean. In these two poems he expresses the spirit of place with aptness and insight.

11. CENTRAL EUROPE

The people of central Europe (the Danubian basin and South Germany), being far from the sea, are possessed by a sort of inner darkness, the darkness of primitive and haunted forests; they need the fresh wind of foreign ideas and influences.
*Margrave:* petty noble.
*this red haze:* the 'bloody darkness' of the previous line.
*nabobs:* eastern princes (as opposed to the local margrave).

12. STEEP STONE STEPS

A picture of Naples and an experiment in alliterative verse, bringing out the contrast between the poverty and degradation of southern Italy and its warm-hearted, sunny generosity of spirit.
*Dante's derelict daughter:* Constance, daughter of Manfred, King of Naples, was deprived of her inheritance on her father's death. (See *Purgatorio*, Canto III.)
*Peter's pence:* tax imposed by the Roman Catholic Church.

ROY CAMPBELL (born 1901) was born in South Africa, and many of his poems evoke the scenes of his youth. He manages traditional forms with ease and fluency (*The Zebras* is a sonnet), and there is about his work an air of swaggering rhetoric reminiscent of Byron and not common among Campbell's contemporaries. It is impossible not to feel the power and vividness of his descriptive writing. These three poems are all written in praise of natural energy; the first two contain striking metaphors and comparisons, and their highly coloured imagery reminds us of a musical score in which there is a good deal of brass.

E. E. CUMMINGS (born 1894) combines scrupulous craftsmanship with spontaneity. He has developed a highly personal style which to him is completely natural and in anyone else would seem like affectation. Most of his poems are immediate personal observations on life, love, society, people of all kinds. They are not difficult to understand, provided you do not seek to express their meaning in your own words; the more you try to explain them, the more elusive their meanings become. In the following notes I have tried to suggest only some of the ideas to be found in these poems.

### 14.  THE CAMBRIDGE LADIES

*Cambridge:* Massachusetts, home of Harvard College.

### 14.  WHAT IF A MUCH OF A WHICH OF A WIND

A rhapsody on the human spirit. Even if a mighty wind should blow the world upside-down the human spirit will still be the secret of the universe. Whatever happens to the world, those 'whose hearts are mountains, roots are trees' will always greet the coming of spring. The more you and I are destroyed by the incalculable future, the more we shall live.

### 15.  IT'S OVER A (SEE JUST

The lesson we learn from the apple orchard is that between birth and death it is man's nature to act, even though acting may be a form of stealing. You and I have stolen our experience, and the world ('they') makes us pay for it.

*gravensteins:* an American apple of fine flavour and beautiful appearance.

### 16.  YOU SHALL ABOVE ALL THINGS BE GLAD AND YOUNG

Youth and happiness are the qualities of a good life. Love is the only necessity, and love gives me a sense of increased space and decreased time. Do not *think*; do not be anxious about the future, for that is the beginning of knowledge, as progress is the beginning of death. I can learn wonder from a bird's song, just as too much speculation can destroy the mystery of the stars.

W. H. DAVIES (1871–1940) wrote hundreds of short poems, and in the 1920's was admired for the wrong ones—for those which suited the taste of the anthologists. Later critics have undervalued his poems because they are not clever or complex. He was always short of money and wrote too much, yet a strain of pure poetry, simple and unsentimental, runs through his work; he can be wryly humorous about himself (as in the first of these poems) or unaffectedly tender in the expression of feeling (as in the other two).

WALTER DE LA MARE (1873–1956).

### 19. THE BEAD MAT

An emotional situation conveyed by suggestion rather than direct statement. The speaker does not respond to the girl's love-gift, and the 'beaten ship' which he seems to see in her eyes is a symbol of her despair.

### 20. THE FECKLESS DINNER PARTY

A dramatic rendering of a fantastic incident in which a group of purposeless society diners-out are led down into hell by a mysterious new butler. Notice the contrast between the jerky inanities of the diners' conversation and the measured smoothness of the final descriptive lines.

EMILY DICKINSON (1830–1886) lived the life of a recluse in her father's house at Amherst, Massachusetts. She was in love at least once but did not marry; she had an almost morbid dislike of publicity and even of society. Her poems were neglected and almost unknown until after her death. It is only recently that she has come to be recognised for what she was—a poet of timeless and original genius whose precision, economy and even dryness of statement ally her to modern movements in poetry rather than to her mid-Victorian contemporaries.

She may be said to have found her style ready-made: the only recognisable influence on the form of her poems comes from the hymns she was brought up on. Some of her work was as sentimental as the worst of evangelical hymns, but it underwent little revision or selection, and many poems which she would have destroyed on reconsideration have survived her. On the other hand, her inspired work strikes us as that of a natural poet of the same dazzling purity as Blake was in his most admired lyrics.

*I taste a liquor never brewed* expresses with almost startling directness her sense of ecstasy in mere existence. *The sky is low, the clouds are mean* shows her to be no sentimentalist about nature, which indeed has its moments of meanness. *A narrow fellow in the grass* recaptures the combination of fascination and horror produced by the sight of a snake. *I heard a fly buzz when I died* presents an intuition of the onset of death, which appears as something small, like a fly, interposed between her and the light, and growing until it blots out the whole of consciousness. *Faith is a fine invention* exemplifies the keen wit which seldom deserts her even at her most ecstatic, and which connects her both with the seventeenth century and with modern poetry.

## T. S. ELIOT (born 1888).

### 25. THE LOVE SONG OF J. ALFRED PRUFROCK

The title poem of Eliot's first book, published in 1917. Apart from its intrinsic merits it has been of immense importance as exemplifying an entirely original poetic method. Eliot comes to poetry as a man whose mind is saturated with the whole tradition of European culture from the classical times onwards. His poems are rich in suggestion and allusion: literature, art, and theology—as well as, and of equal importance with, personal observation and experience—are assumed as a background. The more of this background we are familiar with, the more we shall find in his work.

Nevertheless, a first approach must be made by way of the poems themselves. They mean, on the whole, what we think they mean as we read them. If we ask ourselves, 'What does Prufrock mean?' we must look primarily to our own responses for an answer. Without expert knowledge we can see that the poem is a dramatic monologue by a self-conscious, timid, respectable man approaching middle age who has not the courage to propose love to the woman he desires. He is also something of a social snob. The tone is partly one of romantic rhetoric, partly mock-heroic. It is as if the speaker sees himself as a great lover dwindled into a comic and rather pathetic failure. His state of mind is one of pain and tension. He seeks relief from strain in a state of anaesthesia: that is why the simile in line 3 is so important. To quote an American scholar:[1]

'His love song is the song of a being divided between passion and timidity: it is never sung in the real world. For this poem develops a theme of frustration, of emotional conflict, dramatised by the "you and I".'

The same writer points out that the 'you' of line 1 is the speaker's other self—the passionate self submerged by the self of convention. The epigraph from Dante may be translated:

'If I thought my answer were to one who ever could return to the world, this flame should shake no more. But since none ever did return alive from this depth, if what I hear be true, without fear of infamy I answer thee.' (*Inferno:* Canto XXVII, 61–67. Temple Edition.)

In other words, the experience related in the poem can be spoken of only because it will never be revealed in the world of the living.

### 30. ANIMULA

The title, borrowed from the Emperor Hadrian or from Dante, means 'the little soul'. The poem is an account of the progress of the soul from the time when it leaves the creator's hand in a state of innocence until, corrupted by desire, frustration and self-will, it ends in misery and violence, to live again only after the death of the body.

*running stags:* foreshadowing the fate of Actaeon suggested later by the mention of the imaginary Floret. In pursuit of Diana, Actaeon was changed to a stag and destroyed by his hounds.

*imperatives:* natural impulses come to conflict with moral necessity, free fantasy with actuality.

*Encyclopaedia Britannica:* unable to adjust itself to reality, the growing soul takes refuge in the accumulation of knowledge.

*Guiterriez, Boudin:* imaginary characters, victims of the desire for knowledge and power.

### 31. LINES FOR AN OLD MAN

A portrait of an old man, said to have been intended to represent the French poet, Stéphane Mallarmé (*d.* 1898).

WILLIAM EMPSON (born 1906) studied mathematics and literary criticism while at Cambridge, and wrote this and other striking poems as an undergraduate. His work is witty, complex in meaning, and difficult

[1] George Williamson: *A Reader's Guide to T. S. Eliot* (New York: The Noonday Press, 1953), to which readers are referred for a lengthy discussion of *Prufrock*.

to understand. It owes something to the Metaphysical school of poetry founded by Donne.

The notes on *To an Old Lady* are the author's own. The poem is in honour of an actual person (so the poet assured me) who represents a way of life aristocratic and almost extinct. Yet we of the present generation should not presume either to help or to judge her; we can only observe and revere what she stands for while it lasts.

### 32. TO AN OLD LADY (Author's notes)

First three words from *Lear*. *Our earth* without a god's name such as the other planets have is compared to some body of people (absurd to say 'the present generation') without fundamental beliefs as a basis for action. When a hive needs a new queen and the keeper puts one in the bees sometimes kill her. *Her precession* is some customary movement of the planet, meant to suggest the dignity of 'procession'. The inconfined surface of her sphere is like the universe in being finite but unbounded, but I failed to get that into the line.

## D. J. ENRIGHT (born 1920).

### 33. UNIVERSITY EXAMINATIONS IN EGYPT

A good example of a kind of modern poem consisting of more or less unadorned reporting of some unusual experience. The poet muses on the contrast between the feverish struggle of the young Egyptian examinees to qualify for diplomas and the real nature of the poets whose works are the subject of the examination.

'*Falstaff indulged in . . .* ': this and the following line are howlers perpetrated in the literature paper. *Doolittle* is the dustman in Shaw's *Pygmalion*. *The Yellow Book* was the literary and artistic magazine of the 1890's, a century after the death of Dr. Johnson.

*tric-trac:* gambling game resembling backgammon.

*Akhenaton:* a fourteenth century B.C. ruler of Egypt whose religious revolution may have initiated the worship of the sun.

## JAMES ELROY FLECKER (1884–1915) was a poet of great promise who went to the Near East as an official of the Consular Service, but died of consumption in Switzerland.

### 34. TO A POET A THOUSAND YEARS HENCE

*Maeonides:* Homer. In Book I of the *Odyssey* Telemachus defines the right of poets to speak as they please: 'Why grudge our loyal bard the right to speak as the spirit moves him.'

ROBERT FROST (born 1874), for many years America's most popular poet, published his first poems in England in 1915. The son of a New England father and a Scottish mother, he has spent most of his working life, as poet and farmer, in the bleak and hilly country near the north-eastern seaboard of the U.S.A.

His poems have achieved a wide popularity because of their faithful revelation of the life of the farming people of Frost's country, their shrewd and homely wisdom, and a simplicity concealing depths of thought and feeling.

### 35. THE TUFT OF FLOWERS

Many of Frost's poems are about the sense of community he feels with other people, even those who are absent. He never sees the mower, but the butterfly leads him on where the mower has been before and shows him the tuft of flowers he has spared. The poet at once sees this as a 'message', and his sense of isolation from his fellow-worker vanishes.

### 37. MENDING WALL

The mood of this poem is a combination of ruefulness at his neighbour's unneighbourly insistence on keeping the wall in good repair, and a mischievous glee at the way in which 'something' damages it each winter. The 'something' can only be *frost*: the poet is punning on his own name. To him community between men is the civilised way of life; and as his neighbour grasps a boulder and holds it aloft, he seems like a savage dwelling in the darkness of ignorance and mistrust. The subtlety of the poem comes from the play of different moods across its surface—loneliness, annoyance, and humour.

### 38. TOO ANXIOUS FOR RIVERS

Human life is like a river: there is no need for anxiety as to the origin and destination of either. Whatever Indian or Roman philosophers may have said about the origin and purposes of life, we can only be sure that it is love.

*Lucretius:* Roman poet (first century B.C.), expounded the philosophy of Epicurus (341–270 B.C.).

## DAVID GASCOYNE (born 1916).

### 39. SNOW IN EUROPE

In autumn 1938 the ambitions of Hitler and the Nazis were temporarily satisfied and war averted for a year by the betrayal of Czechoslovakia at

Munich by Neville Chamberlain's policy of appeasement. In this poem, which is an imaginative reflection on politics, the mood of stunned but apprehensive relief which followed the signature of the Munich agreement is symbolised by the continent-wide snowfall. As the last lines of the poem prophetically suggest, when the mood passed the outbreak of war was terrible.

ROBERT GRAVES (born 1895) has been publishing poems for forty years—mostly short, often witty, always of scrupulous economy of statement. His subject-matter is as varied as life itself, and he is equally admired for love poems, poems on mythological subjects, and satires.

### 40. LOST ACRES

Certain 'lost acres' stubbornly refuse to be mapped each time there is a new ordnance survey. They are accounted for only by 'intercalation', a process whereby measurements are inserted on maps by means of intelligent guesswork.

The mind contains similar unexplored regions, beyond the reach of introspection. There is no reason to suppose that these regions are full of primeval monstrosities; they may be full of pleasant things. To explore such a place would be senseless.

### 41. ON DWELLING

This poem describes a state of mind in terms of a landscape. The poet feels himself to be an inhabitant neither of the countryside nor of the town. He is actually living in the town but feels no sense of community with its inhabitants, who are more like ghosts than people.

### 41. THE POETS

Distinguishing between good and bad poets should be no more difficult for the critics (the 'unthrifty writers') than picking out a good bargain or a good servant is for an honest housewife. The critics seem to lack the housewife's discrimination.

### 42. THE GREAT-GRANDMOTHER

A portrait of the ultimate wisdom, the proud self-sufficiency of extreme old age as exemplified in a matriarch of the well-to-do classes. Compare this poem with *To an Old Lady* (William Empson).

### 43. LOLLOCKS

Lollocks is the name invented by the poet to denote all the petty annoyances which result from one's own sloth and unhappiness.

THOMAS HARDY (1840–1928). The poems for which Hardy is remembered with most admiration are mostly short, deeply felt, often odd and irregular in language and form. Almost everything he wrote bears the stamp of his highly individual personality and genius: he had no use for conventional phrases and conventional thoughts. His attitude to life was a mixture of acceptance and resentment, anger and amusement. Poetry was the means of expressing these varying moods as they were induced by his own experience, whether present or remembered. Wordsworth wrote of poetry as originating in 'emotion recollected in tranquillity'; Hardy's poems often seem to spring from tranquillity recollected in emotion. Again and again he looks back to the past, as the source of former happiness and the key to the understanding of later sorrow and disillusion.

Hardy's individuality in form and diction has been mentioned; but what gives his poems their unique quality is, to an even higher degree, their very personal rhythms. Although he uses traditional metrical verse-lines, he marks each with the accent of his own voice; so that when we read his poems, whether aloud or to the inward ear, we have the feeling that we are listening to the poet himself. This of course is true, in some degree, of all good poetry; but of Hardy it is supremely true.

### 45. I LOOK INTO MY GLASS

An expression of the pathos of diminishing physical strength without any diminution of sensibility.

### 46. AT A LUNAR ECLIPSE

In a partial eclipse of the moon the poet wonders how the whole of human misery and greatness can be represented by the smooth and symmetrical shadow on the moon's surface. The part of the earth whose shadow can be seen stretches from one of the poles to the Central Sea (Mediterranean).

### 47. THE SELF-UNSEEING

The key to the feeling expressed in this poem is the last line. Something was lacking in the serene happiness of that experience of long ago, because those who took part in it were unaware of themselves.

### 48. AFTER A JOURNEY

The poet revisits the scenes of his early life with the woman he loved. In later life they were estranged, and now she is dead; but her ghost leads him back to the scene of their happiness.

Beneath the plain, almost dry statements of this poem can be discerned a note of profound despair—the despair of the materialist. As so often with Hardy, the intention of the poem lies in what is not said, rather than what is. To the believer, it is the soul which is the permanent thing in man: to Hardy, in the mood of these lines, it is merely the face.


JOHN HEATH-STUBBS (born 1918).

### 51 .  DON JUAN MUSES

Many contemporary poems are comments on art and literature. Here the poet tries to enter the mind of a character who interested writers as different as Byron, Browning and Shaw. The finest realisation of the character is Mozart's, in his opera *Don Giovanni*.

Don Juan, the heartless seducer in the Spanish legend, murdered the Commendador of Seville, father of Donna Anna, whom Don Juan had attempted to seduce. The story ends when the Commendador, as a stone statue, visits Don Juan at supper and leads him away to Hell.

*Francis or Dominic:* Franciscan or Dominican friars in their coarse, stiff habits.

*the Day of the Dead:* All Souls' Day.


GERARD MANLEY HOPKINS (1844–1889). Working in almost total isolation, Hopkins achieved during his lifetime no recognition of his genius. It was not until forty years after his death that the startling originality and profundity of his poems was generally realised. On becoming a Catholic and a Jesuit, he renounced all poetic ambition, breaking his silence at length with a long elegy entitled *The Wreck of the Deutschland* (1875). Thereafter he wrote poems as the spirit moved him, but considered poetry as being subordinate to his life's work as priest and teacher. His originality, both in diction and in rhythm, sprang from a distaste with the conventions of Victorian poetry, which were inadequate to express his highly individual reactions to the experience of the senses and the spirit. The moods of his poems vary between ecstatic praise of the natural world and intense despondency at the frustrations of his personal life. He derived peculiar satisfaction from compressing his thought within the limits of the sonnet form, which indeed he adapted and expanded into a characteristically flexible

*Jirighgate to Baliol, Oxford.*

114

*Revera into English Poetry 1918*
*Popularised in 1930.*

*Not a happy man*

instrument. The three sonnets here given exhibit Hopkins in three typical moods.

## 52. THE STARLIGHT NIGHT

The contemplation of the stars in all their multitude and brilliance suggests a series of ecstatic similes. Then the poet asks, 'What is the price of a true love and understanding of the beauty of the universe?' The answer is, 'Prayer, patience, alms, vows'. The stars are the boundaries of Christ's own home.

*whitebeam:* small tree with silvery underleaf.
*abeles:* white poplars.
*shocks:* sheaves of corn.

## 53. THE WINDHOVER

In 1879 Hopkins described this poem as 'the best thing I ever wrote'. The windhover (*o* short as in 'proverb') or kestrel appears to Hopkins as the symbol of Christ himself. The poem is highly complex and has produced a flood of critical explanation. The following rough paraphrase gives part at least of its significance.

'This morning I caught sight of morning's darling, prince of daylight's kingdom, a falcon drawn against the dappled dawn, riding upon the level steady air which rolled beneath him, and striding aloft—I saw how he seemed in his ecstasy to hang upon his rippling wing like one pulling on a rein! Then off he flew like the heel of a skate sweeping round a bow-shaped curve: his plunging and gliding seemed to push back the wind. My heart, unseen, responded to his achievement and mastery. At this point (where the falcon turns) your animal beauty, your valour, and your action (Hopkins is now apostrophising both the falcon and Christ) seemed to bend or buckle, O air and pride and plume! and the fiery red dawnlight which then is reflected from you, O my prince, is a billion times lovelier than ever! and no wonder, for the mere plodding of a plough-horse makes a ploughshare gleam as it cuts the furrow; and the cold grey-blue embers of a dying fire, O beloved one, as they fall, split open and reveal a gash of red-hot gold.'

## 54. I WAKE AND FEEL THE FELL OF DARK

This is probably one of four sonnets referred to in a letter to his friend Robert Bridges, in which Hopkins says, 'Four of these came like inspirations unbidden and against my will. And in the life I lead now, which is one of a continually jaded and harassed mind, if in any leisure I try to do anything I make no way—nor with my work, alas! but so it must be.' (?1885).

Here the poet expresses most powerfully and painfully a bitter self-hatred. He wakes at night and feels the darkness of this emotion suffocating him like the hide of an animal. It is, he says, the will of God that he (Hopkins) must leave a bitter taste in his own mouth. His bones, flesh and blood, as if accursed, are like heavy dough soured by his own sour spirit.

*dead letters:* undeliverable letters (at Post Office). It was one of the bitterest features of Hopkins' spiritual agony of this period that he felt as if Christ were completely withdrawn from him.


A. E. HOUSMAN (1859–1936) published only two volumes of lyrics during his lifetime, one in 1896 and the other in 1922. The popularity they achieved is one of the reasons why his fame has suffered in recent years; and his influence on the poetry of others was not all for the best. But he was a true poet: his feeling, though perhaps narrow, was intense, and his craftsmanship was scrupulous. He was a classical scholar specialising in Latin poetry; terseness of statement and control of emotion are ideals he learned partly from his classical models.

### 54. HER STRONG ENCHANTMENTS FAILING

This poem is included because of its powerful suggestion, though I would not like to have to explain it. Possibly we are not intended to divine a precise meaning. 'The Queen of air and darkness' is obviously Hecate or the moon-goddess. She is at the young man's mercy, but foretells his destruction not long after her own.

*limbecks:* retorts.

### 55. WHEN FIRST MY WAY TO FAIR I TOOK

A characteristic reflection on the irony of fate and the human weakness of vainly wishing that things are otherwise than they are.

### 55. TELL ME NOT HERE, IT NEEDS NOT SAYING

Housman here expresses what most lovers of Nature discover—that she is utterly indifferent. He never excelled this poem in descriptive force.

### 56. FANCY'S KNELL

*Abdon under Clee, Wenlock Edge:* in Shropshire, the scene of most of Housman's poems.


ELIZABETH JENNINGS (born 1926) writes short compact poems about the contemporary state of mind, usually in terms of contemporary situations. Her manner is cool and detached, yet her poems never appear impersonal. *The Enemies* conveys the atmosphere of a place invaded peacefully overnight by means of Fifth Column activities — an atmosphere experienced by many during the Nazi invasions from 1939–41.

D. H. LAWRENCE (1885–1930), the son of a Nottinghamshire miner, suffered all his life from consumption, of which he died. Like many consumptives he possessed great nervous energy and vitality. He wrote both prose and poetry, the two often being somewhat mixed. His most characteristic poetic form was a loose, long-lined free verse.

The quality which most distinguishes his writing—and, one might say, his living—was an intense physical awareness of the organic world: men and women, animals, plants. In his writing, men and women take on something of the blind, instinctive life of animals; animals are humanised.

His style is always a direct expression of his mood; he mistrusts craftsmanship, believing rather in trying to get his intuitive feelings down on paper as nearly as possible in their raw state. Thus, many of his poems seem more like rapid sketches than finished works of art.

### 61. SNAKE

*carob:* tree with large leaves occurring in Mediterranean countries.

*albatross:* from *The Ancient Mariner*, here used as a symbol of guilt requiring expiation.

ALUN LEWIS (1915–1944), a Welsh poet of great promise, was killed at Arakan in Burma, fighting against the Japanese.

### 65. IN HOSPITAL: POONA

Lying sleepless in an army hospital in India, the poet thinks of his wife in Wales. His sorrow at their separation is given world-wide dimensions as he thinks first of the darkness and then of the daylight between India and Wales. (Neither the 'sixty degrees of longitude' nor the 'ten thousand miles of daylight' is geographically exact.)

C. DAY LEWIS (born 1904) is in many respects one of the most representative of the generation of poets who emerged from Oxford at the same time as W. H. Auden. Day Lewis was succeeded as Professor of Poetry at Oxford by Auden. Thus the revolutionaries of yesterday become the academics of to-day!

## 66. NEARING AGAIN THE LEGENDARY ISLE

This is a kind of poem very fashionable in our time—the reconstruction of an incident in classical mythology in the modern idiom. Ulysses' sirens have become mere chorus-girls crooning a theme-song.

LOUIS MACNEICE (born 1907) is a poet of considerable fertility whose gift for spontaneous lyrical utterance sometimes degenerates into journalistic slickness; but if he can be over-clever, he is not inclined to pretentiousness or self-inflation.

## 67. BROTHER FIRE

In this address to the fires which raged during the London 'Blitz' of 1940, the poet sees this elemental force as to some extent expressing even its victims' urge to destroy: though our enemy, fire is also our brother.

## 68. ENTIRELY

We can never understand the whole of life: all we can do is to appropriate some fragments of the ideas of great thinkers. If any one love were wholly satisfying, we should be free from fear and desire. If life were simple instead of a mass of confused sensations, we might have a clear purpose: on the other hand, we might be merely bored.

CHARLES MADGE (born 1912) is a poet never satisfied with conventional forms and phrases. His work is often difficult, but his meaning always worth looking for.

## 69. FORTUNE

Beauty in nature, in art, or in human achievement is what is permanent; we, ordinary mortals, are mere passing vapours unless the chance wind of love blows upon us and reveals our true nature.

EDWIN MUIR (born 1887) is one of the most distinguished of living poets, and his work has been of consistently high quality. One of its recurrent themes is that of man's loss of innocence, not so much morally as in his incapacity to apprehend experience in its original purity and immediacy.

In *Merlin* he asks the enchanter whether any man will ever be able to retrace humanity's steps since the Fall, recover his lost innocence, and destroy time.

*The Animals* are seen by the poet as embodying the state of primal innocence: for them the day on which they were created has remained for ever the same. The following day man was created and, by giving things names, began history. By inventing language man developed memory and so defied death; but in doing so he lost the pure apprehension of experience enjoyed by animals.

WILFRED OWEN (1893–1918). Probably no poet of greater promise has ever died in battle. Owen was killed on November 4, 1918, exactly a week before the armistice. When World War I broke out in 1914 there was a wave of patriotic and idealist sentiment, but when the horrors of an apparent stalemate in the trenches were fully experienced by the men at the front a revulsion occurred, and poets such as Siegfried Sassoon and Wilfred Owen set out to make people at home aware of their sufferings. Owen's poetry is full of pity and horror; at the same time he was a conscious craftsman, and his experiments had considerable influence on later poets such as W. H. Auden and C. Day Lewis.

### 72. DULCE ET DECORUM EST

A description of a gas attack is made the occasion for a bitter denunciation of patriotic propaganda of the kind exemplified in the line from Horace (*Odes*, III, ii, 13)—'Sweet and becoming it is to die for one's country'.

### 73. FUTILITY

Not only is Owen brooding on the futility of a life destined to end prematurely, he is experimenting in a combination of rhyme and assonance. (Read in order the final syllable in each line.) He seems to have felt that assonance (near-rhyme or half-rhyme) expressed a sense of incompleteness and frustration.

Michael Roberts commented as follows: ' . . . Owen, in the second stanza of *Futility*, retards the movement of the first four lines by punctuation and intricacy of syntax, so that the fifth line, unimpeded, comes out with a terrific force, continued, though less vigorously and a little more slowly, as though one added a conclusive afterthought, in the final couplet.'

EZRA POUND (born 1885) was one of the leaders of an Anglo-American literary movement known as 'Imagism', which sprang up just before World War I. It aimed at producing poetry which should be precise and economical, not vague and wordy like much of the poetry of the time. Pound was of considerable importance, not only for his own poems, but for his direct influence on other young poets. T. S. Eliot has always acknowledged him as his master.

74. A PACT

Walt Whitman, whose *Leaves of Grass* appeared in 1855, was the first consciously nationalist poet of the American democracy. He wrote in free verse. As a poetic experimenter of a later generation Pound here confesses to having detested Whitman, to whom, however, he is now reconciled.

75. SALUTATION

A typical attack on convention and respectability.

FRANK TEMPLETON PRINCE (born 1912). Born in South Africa, F. T. Prince graduated at Oxford, and has since remained in England. He has published two small volumes of poetry, notable for deep but controlled feeling and fastidious precision of language.

KATHLEEN RAINE (born 1908), whose early training was scientific rather than literary, is concerned with human experience in its permanent forms, not in its accidental or political manifestations. The intense and visionary quality of her writing at its best recalls her concern with the poems of Blake.

JOHN CROWE RANSOM (born 1888). Like most American poets Ransom is 'regional' in background. (Frost's background is Vermont and New Hampshire; Cummings' New York and Boston.)Where they are localised (e.g. *Dead Boy*) his poems spring from the southern states with their aristocratic, almost feudal tradition. Ransom is a traditionalist working within regular and well-defined verse forms. His rhythms are deliberate and leisurely, suggesting perhaps something of the slow drawl of Southern speech. His themes are also traditional—love, death, separation, the wilfulness of old age. *Piazza Piece* is a variation on the theme of 'Death and the Maiden'; *Blue Girls* is a variation on the theme of 'Gather Ye Rosebuds'. His great force and originality are to be found in his diction, which consists of a conscious blend of pedantic, even archaic, words with homely and colloquial ones. Notice 'middling' in *Old Man Playing with Children* (verse 5), 'parsnips' at the end of *Winter Remembered*; and the phrase 'a pig with a pasty face' in *Dead Boy*.

### 80. DEAD BOY

The late-born child of an ancient Virginia family has died as the result of sudden illness, or possibly crime. The boy had not been liked, but now that he is dead the county people regard his death as an affront to their pride.

*bruit:* gossip.

## LYNETTE ROBERTS (born 1919).

### 81. THE SEASONS

A traditional theme treated in a characteristically modern way—in free, unrhymed verse and language which combines words of sensuous and of intellectual appeal.

*contrawise:* i.e. returning, towards winter.

## SIEGFRIED SASSOON (born 1886). Siegfried Sassoon's reputation as a writer of bitterly satirical war poems during World War I has tended to obscure the worth of his lyric writing.

### 82. DEVOTION TO DUTY

The incident of David and Bathsheba retold as if by a modern war correspondent. (See *Samuel II*, Chapter 11.)

### 83. BREVITIES

Line 4. *it:* i.e. his opinion of the world.

### 84. GLORIA MUNDI

*wisdom narrows:* our wisdom seems to be of smaller compass when the Saxon burial-mounds show us what becomes of human effort.

## MARTIN SEYMOUR-SMITH (born 1928).

### 84. GREEN WALL MY GRAVE

A nostalgic elegy in the barracks of an army training centre.

*our enemies the flowers:* the flowers were evidently used as convenient material for bayonet practice.

EDITH SITWELL (born 1887). The poetry of Dame Edith Sitwell has always been remarkable for its brilliant, jewelled surface, and under the surface there are suggestions of intense and profound visions of human life. It would perhaps be a mistake to enquire too closely into the precise significance of these visions. A poem such as *Girl and Butterfly* inevitably calls to mind Coleridge's dictum that 'poetry gives most pleasure when only generally and not perfectly understood.'

85. HOW MANY HEAVENS . . .

Author's note. ' . . . The Stancarest will needs have God not only to be in everything, but to be everything, that God is an angel in an angel and a stone in a stone, and a straw in a straw.' John Donne, Sermon VII.

86. GIRL AND BUTTERFLY

Author's note. 'How butterflies and breezes move their four wings.' Sir Thomas Browne, *The Garden of Cyrus*.

STEPHEN SPENDER (born 1909). His best poems, confessional in character, are representative of their time, and express a sense of guilt at the failure of well-to-do intellectuals to play a part in the struggle of the working-classes towards happiness. It was this feeling which led some of the intellectuals in the 1930's to associate themselves with communism.

DYLAN THOMAS (1914–1953). Dylan Thomas was a highly original poet, appearing to owe little to any predecessor except Gerard Manley Hopkins. He has been hailed as a successor to the bardic tradition of his native Wales, and it is significant that he gave frequent public readings of his poetry. The following quotation from a lecture [1] on Welsh poetry has some application:

> 'In all Welsh bardic poetry, even down to Huw Morus in the seventeenth century and beyond, it was a fundamental principle that in verse sound is as important as sense. This poetry was written to be sung or recited, and the hearers must be delighted by the chime and clash of rhyme and alliteration. Sound being equally important with sense, the latter could on occasion be neglected; and phrases were inserted, in the loosest possible relation to the context, in order to help the metrical effect.'

---

[1] Sir H. Idris Bell: *The Nature of Poetry as Conceived by the Welsh Bards* (Oxford).

This is the portrait of an old hunchback who read his newspaper all day in the public park when the poet was a child. The old man is mocked and pursued by truant boys playing at being tigers or sailors. In fantasy, however, he conjures up a woman, perfect in form, as the presiding deity in the park and in his private mental world. She serves as a compensation for his own defects. The public park may be said to stand for the everyday world in each man's mind, which is peopled with the imaginary figures of his fantasy.

### 91. FERN HILL

A rhapsody on the poet's childhood—a time of innocent joy and well-being, like Adam's life before the Fall. The child is glad because he is unaware that he is in chains, a prisoner whom Time will inexorably lead away from innocence. The poem is not conventionally grammatical, but the sense is not hard to follow if we are prepared to respond to our first impressions and not attempt precise intellectual anaylsis. For example, the line, 'And honoured among wagons I was prince of the apple towns' should convey to the inward eye the picture of a boy riding high on a farm wagon between heavily laden apple trees.

Examples of Thomas's typical stylistic effects are:

(1) Striking metaphorical epithets—e.g. 'the lilting house', a house that appears to be singing because the child looking at it is happy. 'The whinnying green stable'.

(2) Conventional phrases renovated by a slight twist—e.g. 'all the moon long', 'happy as the heart was long'.

(3) Compound adjectives—e.g. 'house high', 'swallow thronged'.

(4) Inversion of normal word order—e.g. 'that take me time would'.

EDWARD THOMAS (1877–1917). As a poet of the English countryside Edward Thomas has affinities with Edmund Blunden, Andrew Young, and Robert Frost, whom he befriended when Frost came to England from America in 1913. There is little that is purely objective or impersonal about his best work. This is charged with intense personal feeling, whether about his own situation or about others. One of the most insistent themes in his later work is that of the war which broke out in 1914. At that time Thomas was 37, and could, as his friend Walter de la Mare has said, honourably have stayed out of the war. But the fate of the men at the front oppressed him so much that he threw aside literary ambition and went to fight. He was killed in Flanders in 1917.

## 93. TEARS

Certain experiences affect us deeply even to the point of tears. Two such experiences are linked in this poem. But what is the real subject? This is, surely, the poet's sadness at the drying up of emotion in himself: things that would once have moved him no longer do so.

## 94. FEBRUARY AFTERNOON

The experience here re-created is that of a sudden sense of the unreality of time. The poet feels as if he were linked with the whole of past and future—an eternity in which there is perpetual war under the eye of an indifferent God.

ARTHUR WALEY (born 1889). Chinese poetry, which had a more or less continuous history from Biblical times until after the Middle Ages, is remarkable for short poems, not long ones. In spite of its differences from western poetry we cannot help feeling how civilised, how modern, how like ourselves were these poets of a thousand years ago and more. To what extent this is due to Arthur Waley's translations I cannot say. Certainly it has been his aim to create, not so much imitations of the original Chinese, which is so strange to our ears, as English poems in free verse. This he has done, paradoxically, by remaining faithful to the meaning of the original and employing his highly sensitive ear in making his versions not merely acceptable but beautiful.

What delights us is the combination of rhythmic subtlety and delicacy with simplicity of language and sincerity and directness of feeling.

Chinese poets did not indulge, as ours do, in a lavish use of picturesque adjectives, and the result, in translation, is increased objectivity. Without being in the least 'atmospheric', these poems convey the essence of a place or a mood in a few vivid and memorable strokes. Neither the language nor the emotion is ever excessive. In a poem such as *The Harper of Chao* the emotion is all the more profound for being restrained. We are always ready to give the Chinese poet credit for feeling more than he says.

## 94. BUSINESS MEN. (Ch'ēn Tzŭ-ang, A.D. 656-698)

A satirical reflection on business men who are so absorbed in material pursuits that they have no time for philosophy.

## 95. ILLNESS. (Po Chü-i, A.D. 772-846)

The son of poor parents, Po Chü-i spent his childhood in Honan and later became a minor government official at Ch'ang-an on the north-western frontier. He was banished to an outlying province for implied criticism of the government. Of his poems Arthur Waley writes: 'No poet in the world can ever have enjoyed greater popularity than Po. His poems were "on the mouths of kings, princes, concubines, ladies, plough-boys, and grooms". They were inscribed "on the walls of village-schools, temples, and ships' cabins".' His aim was always simplicity and freedom from the pedantry which marred the other poetry of his time. He always showed concern for the common people, and for this reason some later Chinese writers regarded his work as vulgar.

*'lan'*: epidendrum.

96. THE HARPER OF CHAO

*gibbon:* small-sized ape.


## WILLIAM BUTLER YEATS (1865–1939)

98. SEPTEMBER 1913

This is one of Yeats' political poems in which he is bitter about the decline in the romantic and chivalrous spirit which had inspired Ireland's struggle against British rule. He contrasts it with the spirit of money-grubbing and superstition which now prevailed.

*O'Leary:* John O'Leary (*d.* 1907) had been a friend of Yeats and was regarded as a patriot of high ideals.

*Edward Fitzgerald, Robert Emmet, Wolfe Tone:* Irish patriots associated with the movement for national independence.

99. SAILING TO BYZANTIUM

Byzantium (Constantinople under the Romans) became for Yeats a symbol of the artistic perfection for which he had been seeking all his life.[1] This was written in 1928 when he was aware of the physical infirmity of old age in the natural world of sensual energy. Nevertheless an old man may have the compensation of a mind which can create and contemplate works of art. He invokes the philosophers and artists of the past to inspire him. They stand in the midst of an unconsuming fire which keeps them pure and inviolate.

*perne in a gyre:* is a private symbol possibly signifying the power of the human spirit to explore the whole of time. He concludes by saying that if he assumes any form after death, it will be that of some perfect work of art fashioned by some Byzantine craftsman.

---

[1] Those interested will find a detailed discussion of the Byzantium poems in *The Lonely Tower* by T. R. Henn (Methuen).

Yeats' own note to this poem reads: 'I have read somewhere that in the Emperor's palace at Byzantium was a tree made of gold and silver, and artificial birds that sang.'

100. STREAM AND SUN AT GLENDALOUGH

A sudden intuition of the pure unthinking life of nature possessed the poet, as if with a sense of being new-born; but the experience was marred by the intrusion of egotistic thoughts. The poem is an illustration of the theme of innocence and experience.


ANDREW YOUNG (born 1885) is perhaps the most fastidious craftsman among modern nature poets. He has published a not very large number of short poems, few of which contain anything like a message, or even any apparent emotion. They are the result of a continuous discipline whose aim is to purify the poet's vision and achieve 'the innocent eye'. The reward of this self-discipline is a kind of poetry which is free from affectation, sentimentality and rhetoric, and which re-creates the English landscape with unequalled brilliance and occasional flashes of wit. Young's achievement is best thought of as an essay in praise.

# INDEX OF TITLES AND FIRST LINES

# ACKNOWLEDGMENTS

The editor and publishers wish to thank the following for their permission to include copyright material in this anthology: Mr. W. H. Auden and Messrs Faber & Faber Ltd, for three poems from *Collected Shorter Poems*, *1930–1944;* Mr. George Barker and Messrs Faber & Faber Ltd, for two poems from *Eros in Dogma*; Mr. John Betjeman and Messrs John Murray Ltd; Mr. Edmund Blunden; the literary Executors of the late Norman Cameron; Mr. Roy Campbell and Messrs Faber & Faber Ltd, for poems from *Adamastor*; Mr. E. E. Cummings; Messrs Jonathan Cape Ltd for poems by W. H. Davies, Robert Frost, Andrew Young; the executors of the late Walter de la Mare; Mr. T. S. Eliot and Messrs Faber & Faber Ltd; Mr. William Empson and Messrs Chatto & Windus; Mr. D. J. Enright and Messrs Routledge & Kegan Paul Ltd; Messrs J. M. Dent & Son for a poem by J. E. Flecker; Mr. David Gascoyne; Mr. Robert Graves; Messrs Macmillan & Co. and the Trustees of the Hardy Estate for eight poems from *Collected Poems*; Mr. John Heath-Stubbs; the Oxford University Press for poems by Gerard Manley Hopkins; the Society of Authors for poems by A. E. Housman; Miss Elizabeth Jennings and Messrs André Deutsch; the Executors of the late D. H. Lawrence; Messrs Allen & Unwin and the Executors of the late Alun Lewis; Mr. Cecil Day Lewis and the Hogarth Press; Mr. Louis McNeice and Messrs Faber & Faber Ltd, for poems from *Collected Poems*, *1925–1948;* Mr. Edwin Muir and Messrs Faber & Faber Ltd, for poems from *Collected Poems*; the Executors of the late Wilfred Owen and Messrs Chatto & Windus; Mr. Ezra Pound; Mr. F. T. Prince and Messrs Faber & Faber Ltd; Miss Kathleen Raine; Mr. John Crowe Ransome; Miss Lynette Roberts and Messrs Faber & Faber Ltd; Mr. Siegfried Sassoon; Mr. Martin Seymour-Smith; Dame Edith Sitwell; Mr. Stephen Spender and Messrs Faber & Faber Ltd; Messrs J. M. Dent & Sons Ltd, for poems by Dylan Thomas; Mrs. Edward Thomas; Mr. Arthur Waley and Messrs Constable & Co. Ltd; the Executors of the late W. B. Yeats and Messrs Macmillan & Co.